Theodore Roosevelt/Spring Rice in WWI, Joshua Barney, Dolley Madison, Elizabeth Monroe, & USN "Airdales"

Daniel Scott Marrone

Copyright © 2016 Daniel Marrone
All rights reserved.

No part of this book may be reproduced in any manner without the written consent of the publisher except for brief excerpts in critical reviews or articles.

ISBN: 978-1-61244-001-9
Library of Congress Control Number: 2016903635

Printed in the United States of America

Published by Halo Publishing International
1100 NW Loop 410
Suite 700 - 176
San Antonio, Texas 78213
Toll Free 1-877-705-9647
Website: www.halopublishing.com
E-mail: contact@halopublishing.com

Acknowledgements and Dedication

My wife, Portia, and daughter, Jamie Ann, are both teachers. Along with performing admirably in the challenging teaching profession, they also provide to me much needed support and patience.

I have been fortunate to have three close friends, who earlier in their lives served in the U.S. Army or New York State Army National Guard. All have retired following lengthy teaching careers. These individuals now donate their expertise and time in fostering an awareness of history. Mr. Marianno "Mike" Ferreira lectures on early Broadway, Jazz, and popular music to senior citizens groups throughout New Jersey. Dr. Aristides "Ari" Scoufelis continues his more than half-century teaching career as an Adjunct Professor of History. He also presents history lectures for the Farmingdale-Bethpage Historical Society. Dr. Alexander T. Short, JD, arranges speaking and tour events for Long Island's North Shore Civil War Roundtable.

The State University of New York provided to me an opportunity to have an excellent academic career. I wish to recognize three of my SUNY colleagues. Dr. W. Hubert Keen is retiring as President of Farmingdale State College at the end of the 2015-2016 academic year. Through his tireless efforts, this college has been positively transformed into a prominent academic institution excelling in the arts and sciences as well as engineering technologies. Professor Ira Stolzenberg began his professional career as a U.S. Coast Guard officer. He then achieved success as a Certified Public Accountant. For many years Ira has served as an educator and department administrator at Farmingdale State College. He also volunteers as Faculty President of the college's chapter of Sigma Beta

Delta International Honor Society. Ms. April L. Orthner was my student at Farmingdale State College, where she graduated with a perfect 4.0 GPA and was the college's valedictorian. She later earned her MBA and now is a high-level credit and financial manager. Ms. Orthner is also a superb adjunct instructor at her *alma mater*, Farmingdale State College.

Much appreciation goes to Ms. Nicole Bedard, Development Coordinator of Beechwood, The National Cemetery of Canada. Through her efforts, British and Canadian government authorities agreed to provide me access to information and photographs regarding the gravesite ceremony honoring Sir Cecil A. Spring Rice in June 2013. Ms. Nancy Stetz is the Education Program Manager of Ash Lawn-Highland, the Home of James and Elizabeth Monroe. Ms. Stetz provided much help in the research on the *first* "First Lady" from New York State: Elizabeth Kortright Monroe.

This book describes American heroes. None of these men or women was perfect as individuals or as decision-makers. Yet, they share at least one common deed. They made the U.S.A. a better nation! One of these American heroes was not an American. Sir Cecil Arthur Spring Rice (SR) was British Ambassador to the U.S. during WWI. His tireless diplomatic efforts during the war were beneficial to his nation, the U.K., and to my nation, the U.S.A. TR and SR were close friends. SR's poignant, poetic words have become a national anthem of the Commonwealth of Nations.

Contents

Chapter 1

Introduction — 7

Chapter 2

Former U.S. President Theodore Roosevelt and
Sir Cecil Spring Rice in WWI; TR's Exceptional Family — 19

Chapter 3

Commodore Joshua Barney: U.S. Naval Hero
of the American Revolution and the War of 1812/
Early American Archivist and Biographer Mary Barney — 78

Chapter 4

Dolley Payne Madison:
"First Lady as the Mother of the Nation" — 94

Chapter 5

Elizabeth Kortright Monroe: La Belle Américain Saves
Adrienne de La Fayette During the French Revolution — 112

Chapter 6

USN "Airdales" in the Pacific Theater of World War II /
USN Air Crewman Wings — 138

Chapter 7

Brigadier General Hugh Mercer: "Jacobite" Rebel
and Hero of the American Revolutionary War — 154

Chapter 8

Martha Washington Visits General George Washington
at the Continental Army Encampments — 166

Chapter 9

Major General Anthony Wayne: "Mad" Warrior
at the Battles of Stony Point and Fallen Timbers   178

Chapter 10

Major General Oliver Otis Howard: Civil War Hero,
Peacemaker, and Founder of Howard University and
Lincoln Memorial University   188

Chapter 1
Introduction

The American Heritage Dictionary of the English Language defines "hero" as: "Any man or woman noted for feats of courage or nobility of purpose; especially one who has risked or sacrificed his/her life." Heroic individuals are not perfect people, but at certain times and for certain purposes they perform heroically. ***Theodore Roosevelt/Spring Rice in WWI, Joshua Barney, Dolley Madison, Elizabeth Monroe, & USN "Airdales"*** provides a collection of nine biographical essays that concisely describe the lives and heroism of *those who have made America a better nation!*

The first essay describes kinships between friends and nations. Cecil Arthur Spring Rice was an English diplomat that served his country and the U.S.A. admirably during WWI. From 1913 to 1918, he was British Ambassador to the U.S. Sir Spring Rice influenced American opinion in favor of joining the Allies fighting *Kaiser* (German Caesar) Wilhelm II and his Imperial armed forces. In the first years of the war, the German army had murdered thousands of innocent Belgian citizens in conquering this small country as well as the northeast region of France. The German navy had sunk hundreds of neutral nation passenger and cargo vessels with the loss of thousands of lives--many of which were Americans. *Kaiser* Wilhelm II had to be stopped! Sir Spring Rice's advocacy for American involvement in WWI mirrored that of former U.S. President Theodore Roosevelt. More than a quarter century earlier, in 1886, the Briton and the American met while voyaging to London on the same ocean liner. Their friendship endured. In 1913, Sir Spring Rice began serving as British Ambassador in Washington, D.C. The Briton warned U.S. President Woodrow Wilson of Germany's massive mobilization for war. The following year, war erupted in Europe and spread to many parts of the globe. Opposing Wilhelm II and the Central Powers, which beginning on November 1, 1914, included the Ottoman Empire, were the Allies: France, Great Britain, and Russia. As Britain's "voice" in the U.S.A., Sir Spring Rice's specific task was to persuade Americans to join the Allies. In strong opposition to U.S. involvement in the war was the huge German American community, Socialist Party adherents, and many isolationist politicians. From 1914 to the beginning of 1917, those opposing U.S. entry into the war were in the majority. However, as the German army and navy perpetrated one atrocity after another, support grew for American intervention in the war. In April 1917, the U.S.A. declared war on Imperial Germany. American "Doughboys" were now fighting at the side of British "Tommies" in the deadly struggle against the German "Huns." The friendship between TR and Spring Rice reflected and helped foster the growing bond between the United Kingdom and the U.S.A. Historian David H. Burton (1976) describes this Anglo-American alliance as follows: "For a long time now, people have spoken of a 'special relationship' existing between the United States and Great Britain, not alone because of blood and institutional ties but due also to the shared experience of great wars." With the U.S. formally joining the Allies in April 1917, Spring Rice's task in America was fulfilled; and he was recalled back to England. Before leaving Washington, D.C. at the beginning of 1918, Cecil Spring Rice, an accomplished poet, revised an earlier poem with a new first verse and title: "I Vow to Thee, My Country." A few weeks later, he traveled to Ottawa en route to London. While in Canada, Sir Spring Rice unexpectedly died on February 14, 1918. Three years later, Spring Rice's poem was set to the music of British composer Gustav Holst. The resultant collaboration is a patriotic hymn *I Vow to Thee, My Country* that is beloved and performed at official ceremonies throughout the Commonwealth of

Nations. This essay concludes with brief descriptions of the lives of TR's family, especially U.S. Army Brigadier General Theodore "Ted" Roosevelt, Jr., a hero at Utah Beach during the June 6, 1944, Normandy Invasion. TR, Jr. was a posthumous recipient of the U.S. Congressional Medal of Honor.

The next essay recalls the bravery of Commodore Joshua Barney—naval hero of the American Revolution and the War of 1812. Born in Maryland, Barney paid a steep price for his forty years of combat fighting the British Royal Navy. *[Now, thankfully, our nations are very close allies!]* Barney was repeatedly wounded in battle. Several times he was taken prisoner and twice made harrowing prison escapes. During the War of 1812, Barney designed, and had constructed by craftsmen, a fleet of shallow-draft, highly maneuverable boats and barges to protect the Chesapeake Bay and the city of Baltimore. On each of these small rowing vessels, Barney positioned a cannon or a mortar. His fleet of vessels was called the *Flotilla*. Unlike Barney's diminutive boats, the deep-draft British ships during this era were unable to venture into the shallow inlets of Chesapeake Bay and Patuxent River. Barney's strategy, therefore, was to attack the British ships and then rapidly row out of reach from these large ships into these shallow inlets. For a number of months in 1814, the Royal Navy was impeded in invading U.S.A. territory by Barney's *Flotilla*. Hugely outgunned, however, the *Flotilla* was eventually destroyed by British ships-of-the-line. With the *Flotilla* eliminated, the British were unimpeded from invading on American soil. On August 18, 1814, the British landed at Benedict, Maryland with the goal of attacking Washington City (later renamed Washington, District of Columbia). American ground forces opened fire on the British, who were headed for the nation's capital. The Americans, at the time, were under the inept command of Brigadier General William Winder. He issued to soldiers and militiamen confusing and contradictory orders. Amidst uncertainty and the battlefield losses of many officers, some American ground forces began fleeing the Battle of Bladensburg—later known derisively as the

"Bladensburg Races." Servicemen who remained on the battlefield were USN Commodore Barney, his sailors, and a contingent of 106 U.S. Marines. They were now fighting on land as infantrymen. Barney's men became the last resistance in defending the capital. Fighting against an overwhelming number of British infantry and Royal Marines, the USN seamen and U.S. Marines sustained terrible casualties. However, these American servicemen refused to cede the battlefield. The Americans fought nearly to the last man! Commodore Barney was shot in the thigh and fell near a cannon. The British sustained significant casualties but finally overran Barney and his men. After the battle, the British found Barney on the ground, severely wounded. Respecting Barney's valor, the commander of the British forces paroled the American commodore to the care of the Royal surgeons. Neither these British doctors nor later their American counterparts were able to locate and remove the bullet from Barney's thigh. His wound caused him constant pain and contributed to his death four years later. Though decimated, Barney's seamen and U.S. Marines delayed the British advance to Washington City. This delay allowed many Americans to escape capture or death when the British ultimately entered and then torched the American capital.

Dolley Payne Madison is the subject of the next essay. President Thomas Jefferson appointed her social hostess during his administration. Later, as First Lady during the Madison Administration, Dolley set a lofty standard for those who have followed in this important role. Early in her life, she was a member of a devout Quaker family. The Payne family first resided in Virginia. When her father encountered financial troubles, he moved the family to North Carolina before moving back to Virginia and eventually settling in Philadelphia. In 1790, Dolley married John Todd and together they had two sons. Three years later, her husband and youngest son perished during a devastating yellow fever epidemic in Philadelphia. Dolley and surviving son, John Payne Todd, then lived with Dolley's mother, Mary Coles Payne. Mrs. Payne transformed the first floor of her home into a boarding house in order to earn much needed cash. Dolley was a comely and statuesque young widow, who invariably attracted the attention of many potential suitors. However, it was brilliant constitutional scholar, U.S. Congressman James Madison, who won Dolley's affection. They were married on September 15, 1794. The shy five-foot, four-inch Madison adored his beautiful bride, who fifteen years later would serve her nation as an extraordinary First Lady. Mrs. Madison initiated in the Executive Mansion (later referred to as The White House) what she termed "Squeezes" that were standing room only social gatherings of senators, congressmen, and diplomats. At these events, her soft-spoken husband chatted with policy makers, who were often persuaded to great effect. During the 1814 British invasion of the nation's capital, Dolley courageously saved an iconic American art treasure. Just before the British Redcoats stormed into the Executive Mansion, she had removed for safekeeping the life-sized Gilbert Stuart portrait of Founding Father George Washington. After the Madison presidency, James and Dolley resided at their plantation called "Montpelier" in Orange, Virginia. James died in 1836 heavily in debt. As a result, Dolley was eventually forced to sell "Montpelier" and lived her final years in the nation's capital. In 1849, Americans of all political parties and regions mourned the loss of Dolley Madison—an individual who was widely admired and embodied the important role of First Lady.

Future First Lady Elizabeth Kortright came from a modestly wealthy Dutch New-York City family that was originally named *van Kortryk*. Her ancestors settled on Manhattan Island in a bustling city originally called *Nieuw Amsterdam*. This American center of commerce and trade later became New-York City (spelled with a hyphen prior to 1898). At age 17, Elizabeth wed U.S. Senator James Monroe, ten years her senior from Virginia. At the close of the 18th century, and intermittently during the first years of the 19th century, James and Elizabeth as well as young daughter Eliza were residing in revolution-torn France. In 1803, while he was chief American diplomat in France, James Monroe assisted in the negotiations led by Robert R. Livingston of New York State for the purchase of the vast Louisiana Territory. About the same time as the purchase, news arrived that the wife of Revolutionary War hero General Marquis de La Fayette was languishing in prison awaiting execution. To effectuate the release of Adrienne de La Fayette, James devised a rescue plan that demonstrated American protection for the French noblewoman. At the risk of losing her life, Elizabeth Monroe volunteered to carry out this plan. She rode in a carriage that had "United States of America" markings. When she was stopped by bloodthirsty Paris mobs, Elizabeth proclaimed that she was visiting a "fellow American" in prison. Elizabeth's selfless act in visiting Madame de La Fayette eventually swayed French public opinion in favor of releasing Adrienne, who otherwise would have been guillotined. Elizabeth possessed exceptional beauty. Thus, the French called her *La Belle Américain*. While in Paris, Elizabeth gave birth to second daughter: Maria Hester Monroe. Unfortunately, during the last two decades of Elizabeth's life, she suffered from chronic rheumatism and seizures--perhaps some manifestation of epilepsy. When her husband was U.S. Secretary of State, and later U.S. president, Elizabeth's illnesses prevented her from fulfilling her social duties. While she dutifully greeted White House guests, Elizabeth rarely made return visits to the homes of these guests. For this, she was criticized and deemed aloof. While she may have been inherently reticent, it was illness that prevented her from making social calls. Thus, her mediocre reputation as First Lady is unjustified. The Monroe presidency ended in 1825. A year later, Elizabeth collapsed in front of a lit fireplace. When she awoke from her seizure, she was seriously burned. She died in 1830 at 62 years of age. Her grief-stricken husband, James Monroe, died just 10 months later at age 73.

The next essay focuses on the U. S. Navy pilots and enlisted aircrews in the Pacific Theater during World War II. The devastating December 7, 1941 multi-wave Japanese sneak attack from the air on Pearl Harbor's "battleship row" and on nearby U.S. Army Air Force Hickam Field resulted in the deaths of 2,403 U.S. Navy, Marine, Army, and civilian personnel. Twenty-one American warships were heavily damaged or sunk in the attack, including eight battleships. Fortunately, the USN Pacific fleet's three aircraft carriers and crews were away at sea during the attack and thus spared to fight another day—and did they! Officers and sailors on all types of USN ships boldly engaged the Japanese navy in enumerable sea and air battles. However, this was the first time in history swarms of carrier-based warplanes dueled in the sky and attacked ships that were sometimes hundreds of miles away from each other scattered across the Pacific. USN flyers fought the Japanese in warplanes specially designed for use on aircraft carriers. Grumman Aircraft Company built many of these warplanes at its Bethpage, Long Island facility. USN pilots engaged in constant combat and, as a consequence, suffered huge loss of life. It is estimated that half of the USN pilots were killed in battle, perished in carrier takeoffs and landings, or drowned by the time they reached their fiftieth mission. The enlisted "Airdales," many of which had the rating "Aviation Machinist Mate," performed tasks that included preparing aircraft for takeoff and repairing planes returning with battle damage. USN Aviation Machinist Mates also served as tail gunners and radiomen in these warplanes. The author's father, Master Chief Petty Officer Aviation Machinist Mate Daniel C. Marrone, was a 32-year veteran of the USN and Naval Reserve. His WWII war record includes serving as a tail gunner on Avenger TBFs fighting in the Pacific. During the Korean War and the early years of the Vietnam War, D. C. Marrone served as a "Flight Crew Chief." Among his many military decorations was the "U.S. Navy Air Crewman Wings"— an honor awarded to enlisted sailors who fought in combat while serving as crewmembers in USN warplanes. He passed away on April 24, 1999. On his gravestone below his name is prominently inscribed: **U.S. Navy E-9 ★★**.

Four Additional Essays

Scotland-born physician Hugh Mercer fled his homeland after the failed Jacobite (followers of James II) Rebellion led by "Bonnie Prince Charlie." Alluding capture, Mercer fled to Philadelphia and initially settled in the western frontier of colonial Pennsylvania. Years later in the French and Indian War, Militia Captain Mercer was wounded and abandoned at Kittanning Village. The stalwart Scot did not give up hope and trod over 100 wilderness miles on foot to reach the safety of Fort Shirley. After the war, Mercer moved to Virginia and established a medical practice and apothecary. During the American Revolutionary War, Continental Army Brigadier General Mercer commanded troops that fought in numerous battles. On January 3, 1777, Mercer faced an onslaught of British Grenadier infantry at the Battle of Princeton. With his horse shot, Mercer fought on foot with sword until being surrounded by Redcoats. Mercer was struck with musket butts on the head and bayoneted seven times. Gravely wounded at Princeton, he clung to life nine days and died on January 12. Hugh Mercer's descendants have included many prominent American military leaders. Most famous were "Blood and Guts" WWII four-star General George Smith Patton, Jr. and highly decorated Major General George Smith Patton III, who fought with valor in the Korean and Vietnam Wars. American musician, composer, and record company executive John Herndon "Johnny" Mercer was also a direct descendent.

Martha Dandridge Washington's love and care for her husband, George, proved to be immensely important to the American Cause for Independence. With her tender support, the General was able to remain with his men in the field for eight years! Decades earlier, Martha was married to Daniel Parke Custis. Following Parke Custis' death, the young widow declined numerous marriage proposals until she met Virginia Militia Colonel George Washington. Upon their marriage, George Washington retired from the militia and lived with Martha and her extended family at Mount Vernon. In the 1775 Continental Congress, Massachusetts representative John Adams nominated Washington as Commander-in-Chief of the, still-to-be formed, Continental Army. That important assignment would span eight exhausting years. During the war, Martha visited and nurtured her beleaguered husband nearly every year at winter army encampments. In undertaking these visits, she would leave

Mount Vernon and repeatedly travel through northeast blizzards and ice storms on primitive roads to join her husband. At these encampments, Martha cared for her hard-pressed husband, who bore the enormous stress of commanding frequently unsupplied and unpaid Continental soldiers. Most important were Martha's visits to the Valley Forge and Newburgh encampments. General Washington described Valley Forge as "a dreary kind of place" that was situated along the frozen Schuylkill River in Pennsylvania. Approximately 2,500 soldiers died from disease, malnutrition, and frigid weather conditions at Valley Forge. Martha's presence not only aided her husband, but she also boosted camp morale with her "let's get to work" upbeat spirit. Martha's lengthy stay at the Newburgh headquarters in Orange County, New York, spanned much of the last 17 months of the war. Her presence at the Newburgh encampment greatly helped her husband during a dangerous interlude (1781-1783) between the victory at the Battle of Yorktown and the signing of the Treaty of Paris. Under the weak Articles of Confederation, Congress was unable to raise money from the various states to pay the now-idled Continental Army soldiers. These soldiers were billeted at the New Windsor Cantonment in Vail's Gate, about five miles from Washington's Newburgh headquarters. Without pay and denied permission to return home, these restless soldiers began to threaten mutiny. The worst of these potential mutinies involved discontented officers. On March 15, 1783, the Commander-in-Chief responded with his celebrated "Newburgh Address." Following his speech, Washington began reading a handwritten letter. He could not read the letter without the aid of eye spectacles. As he was placing the spectacles on, Washington apologized "for growing gray and blind in the service of his country." With this humble apology, George Washington quelled what could have been a catastrophic mutiny of Continental Army officers and soldiers. Martha's devotion to her husband helped—perhaps even enabled--him to persist as battlefield commander throughout the eight-year war and flourish later for another eight years as the first president of the new republic. For this, Lady Washington deserves the nation's great appreciation and respect.

American Major General Anthony Wayne epitomized the definition of "warrior leader." His bravery on the battlefield and his ability to command soldiers were best demonstrated at the July 16, 1779, bayonet raid at Stony Point and at the August 20, 1794, Battle of Fallen Timbers. In both instances, Wayne devised and led a daring, well-executed military plan. With the stunning victory at Stony Point, Wayne thwarted the intentions of British General Henry Clinton in conquering New York's Hudson River Valley. Had Clinton been successful, the British would have invaded northward and subsequently controlled the strategically vital north-south Hudson River waterway that separates the New England states from the rest of the country. Thus, the Stony Point raid was invaluable as it effectively quashed Clinton's plan. In the years following the war, Native American Miami Chief Michinikwa ("Little Turtle") led a confederation of tribes that attacked U.S. settlements in the Old Northwest Territories, especially in the future state of Ohio. In 1790, in an attempt to quell these attacks, Brigadier General Josiah Harmar led U.S. troops in a battle to defeat "Little Turtle" and the Native American confederation. This expedition failed in its mission, and many U.S. soldiers were slaughtered. A year later, Major General Arthur St. Clair led troops in a second effort to overcome the Native Americans. This effort failed as well. Worse yet, the raids on U.S. settlements were escalating. President George Washington assigned Major General Anthony Wayne to make a third attempt to quell these deadly raids upon U.S. settlements. Wayne systematically organized, trained, and equipped his troops that he named the "Legion Army." Leaving their base in the village of Cincinnati, the "Legion Army" fought the Native American confederation fighters at the Battle of Fallen Timbers. Though the "Legion Army" sustained significant casualties, "Little Turtle" and the confederation were defeated and forced to sign the Treaty of Greenville that ceded much land to the U.S. nation. For his exceptional bravery and stunning achievements on the battlefield, Wayne was given the derring-do sobriquet "Mad." U.S. Army Major General Anthony Wayne ranks among the best battlefield commanders in history.

The final essay is on U.S. Army Major General Oliver Otis Howard. He was born in Maine in 1830, and during the Civil War bravely led the Union Army XI Corps. Twice wounded at the Battle of Fair Oaks, Howard's right arm was amputated. For his valor in the Peninsular Campaign, Howard was awarded the U.S. Congressional Medal of Honor. Subsequently, however, his XI Corps soldiers were unexpectedly attacked and routed at the Battle of Chancellorsville on May 2, 1863. Sixty days hence, Howard's XI corps were again routed at the village of Gettysburg and forced to make a fighting retreat south to nearby Cemetery Hill. Eventually, the Union Army defeated General Robert E. Lee's Confederates at the Battle of Gettysburg. Later in the war, Howard served with distinction under "War is Hell!" Major General William Tecumseh Sherman in the climactic victory at the Battle of Atlanta. Following the war, Howard was appointed Commissioner of the Freedmen's Bureau, for which he served from May 1865 until July 1874. Through Howard's tireless efforts, former enslaved African Americans gained social and economic benefits. However, Howard continually faced deep resentment and formidable obstacles from racist political leaders from the North as well as from the South. During his difficult tenure as Commissioner, he established a university that was later named after him. Howard University, located in the nation's capital, is a highly recognized academic institution that prepares individuals in a wide array of professions—especially in the health fields. While on temporary leave from the Freedmen's Bureau, Howard was tasked with suppressing attacks from Native Americans in the Arizona Territory. With only U.S. Army Scout Thomas Jonathan Jeffords, Howard bravely entered Chief Cochise's camp. There, Howard negotiated with Cochise of the Chokonen band of the Chiricahua Apache Nations. After several meetings, the Cochise-Howard Treaty was signed. Howard achieved landmark success in formulating a heretofore-unattainable lasting peace with Cochise and the Apache Nations. Subsequently, however, Howard was unsuccessful in peacefully convincing the Nez Perce Tribes to relocate to a new reservation. The Nez Perce eventually relocated, but only after being defeated in battle by the might of the U.S. Army. In 1896, Howard fulfilled a request, made more than three decades earlier, by then President Abraham Lincoln. Shortly before the 16th president was assassinated, Lincoln asked Howard to help the east Tennesseans, many of whom were loyal to and fought for the Union. Using his own funds, Howard fulfilled Lincoln's request by financially supporting the establishment of Lincoln Memorial University in Harrogate, Tennessee. Howard was brave, honest, humane, and loyal. He most certainly embodied his noble reputation as "The Christian General."

Chapter 2
Former U.S. President Theodore Roosevelt and Sir Cecil Spring Rice in WWI; TR's Exceptional Family

Special Relationship between the U.K. and the U.S.A.

Amidst the horror of World War I, the United Kingdom and the United States of America became close allies. From 1775 to 1783, however, these English-speaking nations were bitter enemies. Trouble began when American colonists rebelled against "Mother Country" Great Britain. The War for Independence lasted from April 1775 to October 1783. Three decades following this conflict, the two nations were again fighting in the War of 1812. The Treaty of Ghent was signed on December 24, 1814. The document stipulated: *status quo ante bellum* ("things stay as before the war"). While no territory was gained or lost by either nation, the treaty obtained something far more important: the start of a lasting amity between the countries. In the twilight of the 19th century, there was a steady "warming of relations" between the nations. During the 1898 Spanish American War, the British sold coal to and permitted re-supply of U.S. Navy ships under the command of Admiral George Dewey at British Royal Navy ports in Asia. The British also persuaded other European nations to maintain neutrality in the Spanish American War, rather than side with the Spanish monarchy. By the beginning of the 20th century, Anglo-American relations evolved into "The Great Rapprochement." In

1946, Sir Winston Churchill referred to this strong bond between these nations as the "Special Relationship between the U.K. and the U.S.A."

Cecil Arthur Spring Rice: Early Career

Two individuals that fostered this bond between nations were Cecil Arthur Spring Rice and Theodore Roosevelt. Spring Rice was born in England on February 27, 1859. He came from a noble family that was English (Spring) and Irish (Rice). Thus, he had a double surname that was spelled without a hyphen. His father was diplomat Honorable Charles William Spring Rice, who was the second son of notable Whig politician Thomas Spring Rice, 1st Baron Monteagle of Brandon. Cecil was a dedicated student at Eton College, an esteemed boys-only school located in Berkshire, England. He then attended and graduated from Balliol College, a component of highly prestigious Oxford University. In 1882, he passed an examination that was required for entry into Britain's Foreign Office. Five years hence, he was appointed 3rd Secretary at the British legation in Washington, D.C. During his years in the U.S.A., the ambitious British bachelor enjoyed the excitement and optimism found in late 19th century America. On November 6, 1886, Spring Rice boarded an ocean liner bound for England. Onboard the ship, *RMS (Royal Mail Ship) Etruria*, was New York State politician Theodore Roosevelt. Spring Rice introduced himself to TR while at sea. They immediately became friends—so much so the brash New Yorker asked "Springy" to be his "Best Man" at his December 2, 1886 wedding to Edith Kermit Carow. The nuptial was held in St. George's Church, located in Hanover Square, Central London. Spring Rice and TR had much in common: literary ability, staunch beliefs in, and a complete willingness to sacrifice for, God and country. Though of different nationalities and temperaments, they were both dedicated to fulfilling moral principles; and both were steeped in patriotic devotion.

Late 1880s photograph of Cecil Arthur Spring Rice
about the time he befriended Theodore Roosevelt.

In 1904, Spring Rice married Florence Caroline Lascelles, the daughter of Sir Frank Cavendish Lascelles. Two years later, Spring Rice was appointed British Ambassador to Iran, a position he held until 1908. While stationed in Iran, the perceptive diplomat kept a watchful eye on Germany's growing militarism. Historian David Henry Burton describes Spring Rice as follows: "Now in 1907, Germany was the rival nation [to Great Britain] most to be feared. An active Germany so well prepared for war was a sobering thought. Spring Rice's often quoted pessimism was in this instance realism of a high order but his plea, along with that of a few other spokesmen, went unheeded" (1990, p. 41). The Briton advocated for military preparedness and for a strong Anglo-American military alliance. In 1908, Spring Rice celebrated the baptism of his son, Anthony Theodore Brandon Spring Rice, in London. "Theodore" in the diplomat son's name was to honor his son's "Baptism Godfather," Theodore Roosevelt. At that time, TR was U.S. President. The two friends excelled in literary endeavors. TR wrote numerous books and articles; Spring Rice composed poetry. The following is one of Cecil Spring Rice's poems:

"Day"

'I am busy' said the sea. 'I am busy.
Think of me making continents to be.'
'I am busy' said the sea.
'I am busy' said the rain.
'When I fall it's not in vain; Wait and you will see the grain.'
'I am busy' said the rain.

'I am busy' said the air.
Blowing here and blowing there, up and down and everywhere.
'I am busy' said the air.

'I am busy' said the sun.
'All my planets, every one, know my work is never done.'
'I am busy' said the sun.

Sea and rain and air and sun.
Here's a fellow toiler-one, whose task will soon be done.

While serving as British Ambassador to Sweden (1908-1912), Spring Rice composed a poem he titled: *"Urbs Dei"* ("The City of God"). The original first verse of this poem was a clarion call to battle. The second verse was a tribute to God. In early 1918, Sir Spring Rice substituted a new first verse and renamed the poem: "I Vow to Thee, My Country." This poem was his utmost expression of patriotism to country and devotion to God. Revised and renamed at the beginning of 1918, his poem serves as an eternal remembrance of those who served their country and paid "the final sacrifice."

TR's "Crowded Moment" Life

Theodore Roosevelt was born in 1858 within New-York City, which was spelled with a hyphen and consisted of only Manhattan Island until 1898. That year, voters of Manhattan and four counties—Kings (Brooklyn), Queens, The Bronx, and Richmond

(Staten Island)—narrowly voted in favor of unifying into "Greater New York City." The hyphen in the city's name was dropped. Over time, the "Greater" and "City" portions of the name became widely understood and are no longer employed except when a distinction is necessary between "New York" the City and "New York" the State. Though TR's sisters, Anna (called "Bamie") and Corinne (called "Conie"), preferred to remain in N-YC, TR opted to live further east on Long Island. TR's red-painted, Victorian-styled home and sprawling north shore estate acres are called: "Sagamore Hill."

TR's earliest ambition was to become a naturalist. However, with the death of his father in 1878, 20-year old TR needed a steady income. Thus, he decided to become a writer. TR certainly achieved this goal throughout his life for he authored 35 books as well as scores of magazine and daily newspaper articles on a broad range of subjects. He also wrote a mountainous amount of official and personal correspondence, estimated to be over 150,000 in number, to individuals from a stultifying collection of nationalities, professions, and talents. The hyperactive TR was always in motion and forever curious about anything animal-related. However, his love for animals did not deter him from shooting extreme quantities of them during his safaris. Though his eyesight was poor, his hearing was exceptionally keen. He maintained throughout his life an uncanny ability to distinguish among the vast array of bird songs. Spring Rice, bemused by TR's abundant childlike energy and never ceasing enthusiasm, made an astute, often-quoted observation about his American pal: "The thing you always have to remember about Theodore is he's about six [years old]."

Many in the Roosevelt extended family were quite "well-to-do" financially. TR's wealth was indeed sizable compared to many lower income Americans, especially the hordes of late 19th century immigrants from eastern and southern Europe who dwelled in crowded tenements barely eking out a subsistence living. Still, TR's inheritance was not inexhaustible. Thus, TR was expected to join in one of the various Roosevelt family business concerns.

Instead, TR entered boisterous and corruption-prone New York politics. At 24, he ran for and was elected to the New York State Assembly as a reform candidate from the Republican Party. He served three one-year terms from 1882 through 1884. TR attained statewide prominence as a transformational activist and spoke forcefully against crooked politicians and sleazy "rotten ward politics." With dedication and verve, he meteorically rose to prominence as the Republican Party leader in the NYS Assembly. Unfortunately, tragedy struck twice on February 14, 1884. On this mournful day, TR's mother, "Mittie," died from typhoid fever and his wife, Alice Hathaway Lee Roosevelt, succumbed to Bright's (kidney) disease. His wife, age 22, had given birth two days earlier to a baby named Alice Lee Roosevelt. On February 14, which ironically was Valentine's Day, TR scratched in his diary an "X" and wrote: "The light has gone out of my life." TR is noted for his robustness, a character trait he exhibited innumerable times. Yet, he suffered from recurring bouts of asthma and from a possible case of bipolar disorder referred to as "Exuberance." Presidential historian Douglas Brinkley (2009) describes Roosevelt's "Exuberance" as follows: "His set of symptoms—propulsive behavior, deep grief, chronic insomnia, and an all-around hyperactive disposition—demonstrate both the manic and the depressive phases of bipolar disorder" (p. 123).

The deaths of his mother and wife rendered TR deeply depressed. He also had to cope with his chronic asthma that was acerbated by stress. He dealt with these emotional and health burdens by exiting bustling Empire State for the stark, unforgiving Dakota Badlands to become a self-reliant hardscrabble cattle rancher. At first, the Dakota cowboys called him "Dandy" and "Four Eyes." However, he surprised everyone with his stamina on horseback and for his never-quitting attitude. The "New York Dude" eventually rustled cattle as if he performed this task all his life. While out west, TR volunteered as a Deputy Sheriff. While TR looked like a bespectacled "Eastern dandy" clad in tailored cowboy outfits, he nevertheless packed a mean punch. TR was a highly proficient boxer. While confronting a *desperado* in a North Dakota saloon, TR knocked the villain to the floor with a skillful "one-two" jab and punch.

Due to severe draughts, blizzards, and other calamities, TR lost much of his inheritance that he invested in cattle ranching out west. However, these financial losses paled in comparison to the benefits he derived from his time as a cowboy. The emotionally distraught New York State politician who ventured out west returned east emotionally focused and confident. TR now turned his attention and energy on becoming a national leader in reform politics and honest government service. He often stated: "I never would have been President if it had not been for my experiences in North Dakota" (http://www.livescience.com/29383-theodore-roosevelt-national-park.html; Retrieved 2/29/2016).

In 1886, Theodore Roosevelt began an astonishing path of increasingly important appointed and elected positions: U.S. Civil Service Commissioner; New-York City Police Commissioner; U.S. Assistant Secretary of the Navy; Spanish American War Lieutenant Colonel and then full Colonel of the U.S. Volunteers Regiment spryly dubbed the "Rough Riders"; New York State governor; and U.S. Vice President. On September 14, 1901, following the tragic assassination death of President William McKinley, TR assumed the U.S. presidency. As the first U.S. president in the 20th century, he made an indelible mark on history through landmark legislation establishing federal government oversight of key American industries that included inspection of food as well as the efficacy and safety of drugs. Notably, he has been deemed a "trust buster" for being the first U.S. president to legally prevail against ruinous monopolies such as John Pierpont Morgan's Northern Securities Company. TR was also responsible for establishing America's national parks and the U.S. National Parks Service. According to Douglas Brinkley (2009), TR's creation of the national parks was the "Wilderness Warrior's" most enduring legacy.

In his landslide November 1904 victory at the polls, TR was elected to serve a second term as U.S. president. At this point in time, TR asserted that he would not seek a third term. Making this rash proclamation was arguably his greatest error of judgment because he thrived as president and—using a well-known TR aphorism—was "Deee-lighted!" in serving as the nation's Commander-in-Chief. During his 7.5 years in the U.S. nation's highest office, TR's achievements were profound and enduring. TR was ranked number *four* out of 43 U.S. presidents in a 2000 poll and number *four* out of 44 presidents in a 2009 poll--both conducted by C-SPAN and reported by NBC Nightly News. The only presidents ranked higher than TR in these polls were Abraham Lincoln, George Washington, and TR's fifth cousin, Franklin Delano Roosevelt. The rankings were those of 65 presidential historians, who assessed U.S. presidents using 10 leadership attributes (http://www.nbcnews.com/id/29216774/ns/politics-white_house/t/list-presidential-rankings/; Retrieved 2/29/2016).

Declining to run for a third term, TR instead tapped a close associate, veteran Ohio trial lawyer and diplomat William Howard Taft, to run as his successor for the nation's highest office. The American electorate concurred with TR's choice. Taft was easily elected to the presidency in November 1908. However, by 1912 TR was deeply veering to the "left" politically as compared to fellow Republican Taft, who was far more politically conservative. With encouragement from an escalating number of liberal Progressives in the nation, TR was urged to enter the 1912 presidential race. That year, TR lashed out at Taft, his rival for the Republican Party nomination, and his Democrat Party opponent, Thomas Woodrow Wilson, in a speech TR called "The Right of the People to Rule":

> The great fundamental issue before the Republican Party and before our people can be stated briefly. It is: Are the American people fit to govern themselves, to rule themselves, to control themselves? I believe they are. My opponents [Taft and Wilson in the forthcoming 1912 presidential race] do not. I believe in the right of the people to rule. I believe the majority of the plain people of the United States will, day

in and day out, make fewer mistakes in governing themselves than any smaller class or body of men, no matter what their training, will make in trying to govern them. I believe, again, that the American people are, as a whole, capable of self-control and of learning by their mistakes. Our opponents pay lip-loyalty to this doctrine; but they show their real beliefs by the way in which they champion every device to make the nominal rule of the people a sham. (Speech at Carnegie Hall, New York City, March 20, 1912.)

In vying for the 1912 Republican Party nomination for U.S. president, Roosevelt attained more primary delegates than "Bill" Taft. However, the "Grand Old Party" bosses chose the more conservative Taft as their candidate for president. TR was enraged with the GOP bosses and, as a consequence, broke from the party. TR ran for president instead as a candidate of the nascent Progressive Party. When asked by news reporters how he felt after a long season of public appearance campaigning, the former U.S. president responded: "I feel as fit as a Bull Moose." From that point forward, the Progressive Party was called "The Bull Moose Party." In the November 1912 presidential election, TR lost to Virginia-born Democrat New Jersey Governor Wilson. TR came in a strong second place surpassing Taft, the GOP candidate who placed a distant third.

Losing the 1912 presidential race was a major disappointment for crestfallen TR. However, instead of dwelling on this setback, TR was spurred to action. His son, Kermit, and he embarked on a thrilling safari expedition in Africa. Their trophy kills of numerous indigenous animals became the core collection of the American Museum of Natural History. In tribute, this prominent museum named its grand exhibition space: "Theodore Roosevelt Memorial Hall." TR also donated specimens to the Smithsonian Institution. TR helped to establish the Smithsonian's Freer Gallery of Art and was a staunch supporter of the U.S. National Museum that presently is called the National Museum of Natural History. In late 1913, TR agreed to participate in an expedition to map Brazil's *Rio da Dúvida* (River of Doubt). The trek through the rain forest was exciting though extremely hazardous. Three of the expedition members perished due to accidents and murder. TR contracted malaria and was injured in his leg. However, TR fulfilled the mission of the expedition—the mapping of the "River of Doubt." In honor of TR's groundbreaking achievement in mapping this treacherous tributary, the appreciative Brazilian government renamed it: *Rio Téodoro Roosevelt*. Returning to America, TR's popularity was as widespread as ever. TR used his copious notes from the expedition to author articles and books. He also began to be concerned about the nation's lack of military preparedness. Surprisingly, considering how far he veered "left" politically in the 1912 presidential election, TR veered far "right" politically in the years leading up to and during the Great War.

Europe Mobilizes for War

Demographically and socially, Europe has always been a volatile mixture of cultures, ethnicities, languages, and religions. In particular, the Balkan Region of southeastern Europe was--and still is--a flashpoint for fixated loathing among three religious groups—Roman Catholics, Eastern Orthodox Christians, and Muslims. Inhabitants of this region communicate in a vast array of Romance, Slavic, and Islamic-based languages. For centuries the devout Catholic Hapsburgs ruled most of the Balkans. Other regions of the Balkans were part of the Islamic Ottoman Empire or the Eastern Orthodox Christian Russian Empire. In thwarting deadly internal insurgencies as well as bulwarking against neighboring empires wishing to encroach upon the Hapsburg's dominions, Austria-Hungary and Germany formed a military pact known as "The Dual Alliance" in 1879. Three years later, Italy joined these nations to form "The Triple Alliance." In response, the French and the Russians, both inimical enemies of the Teutonic Germans and Austrians, formed their own mutual defense accord called "The Dual Entente" of 1892. With much of Europe mobilizing for war,

Great Britain hesitantly joined France and Russia to form a mutual defense pact called *"Le Triple Entente"* of 1907. By 1912, much of Europe was in the throes of what has been labeled "mobilization," a term signaling the preparation for and prelude to war. The underlying causes for war at this time may be traced to fanatical nationalism, centuries-long hatreds over religion and culture, and the clash of encroaching imperial hegemonies. European potentate rulers during this era rode in horse drawn carriages and, some years later, in open cars festooned with the ancient symbols of heraldic family lineage signaling entrenched absolute rule. Imperious as well as imperial, these despotic rulers were keenly eager to grab political power and sovereign territory, regardless of the cost in lives, by using military force against neighboring countries.

Kaiser Wilhelm II

Prussian King *Kaiser* (in English: "Caesar") Wilhelm II (1859-1941) was heir to the awesome power and privilege of the Teutonic House of Hohenzollern. His *Deutscher* name was: *Friedrich Wilhelm Viktor Albrecht von Preußen*. Wilhelm II loathed many European kings and queens. This is ironic due to the fact that quite a few of these monarchs were related to him by bloodline and/or marriage. His mother, Princess Victoria, was the eldest daughter of British Queen Victoria and the German Prince Consort *Albert von Saxe-Coburg und Gotha*. British Queen Victoria called her hair-trigger, quick-tempered grandson "William" rather than the *Deutscher* equivalent: *Wilhelm*. The Prussian King was devoted to his grandmother and was at her bedside when she passed away in 1901. However, neither his love for Queen Victoria nor his half British bloodline could deter Wilhelm II from despising the British in general. In particular, he abhorred his Uncle Bertie, British King Edward VII, who reigned from 1901 to 1910. Wilhelm II's hatred toward the British stemmed from a mishap at his birth. There were complications stemming from his breech birth. The birthing physicians, all British, were required to use forceps that unfortunately caused damage to the newborn's left arm. This resulted in Wilhelm

II having a permanently shortened, muscle damaged, and useless left arm that would cause him embarrassment and engender his hatred towards the British people throughout his life. He would always blame the British doctors for his shortcomings in physical agility. In adulthood, the *Kaiser* exhibited highly erratic behavior and temper tantrums—all pointing toward mental instability. Due to his mental instability, Wilhelm II was exceedingly dangerous because he was King of Prussia, a German principality that was widely feared for its arch militarism. Wilhelm II was also irked by the fact that the British had a navy far superior in numbers to his own fleet. The *Kaiser* was virulently anti-Semitic. In speaking with the Most Reverend J. Lloyd Thomas of London, Wilhelm's wife recalled her husband asserting that "the Jews did him mischief during the Great War and he has not now a good word for them" (http://www.jta.org/1941/06/05/archive/ex-kaiser-dead-at-82-turned-anti-semitic-after-germanys-defeat; Retrieved 2/29/2016). Queen Victoria's grandsons included British King George V, Russian Czar Nicholas II, and Prussian King Wilhelm II.

The grandsons of British Queen Victoria: British King George V, Russian Czar Nicholas II, and Prussian King, *Kaiser* Wilhelm II.

Wilhelm II despised his cousins and exhibited irrational jealousy, paranoiac suspicion, and blatant hostility toward them and the nations they ruled. All this *angst* contributed to the confrontation and fear that was becoming rampant throughout Europe. At that point in time, nearly all of the major European nations were enmeshed in interlocking, opposing military blocs. "The Triple Alliance" members—Germany, Austria-Hungary, and

Italy sought a military strategy for going to war. Prussian Army-schooled General Alfred Graf von Schlieffen (1813-1913) was the individual chosen to prepare such a plan. In simplest terms, the "Schlieffen Plan" called for Germany to first attack archrival France to the west. With France under German control, troops and materiel could then be shifted to the eastern battlefront for attacking Czarist Russia. While the aim of the "Schlieffen Plan" was straight forward, the methods for accomplishing it were not. The "Plan" avoided a direct, extremely costly frontal attack on France at the heavily defended France-German border. Instead, the German army had to first conquer Belgium. Then the Imperial German forces could flank and more easily invade France through the relatively lightly defended Belgium-France border. With control of France, the German military forces could then shift east to attack and occupy Poland. With a German-Austrian military stronghold in Poland, a crushing attack on Czarist Russia could be launched. In 1906, at the age of 93, German Chief of Staff von Schlieffen retired. The *Kaiser* replaced him with General Helmuth Johann Ludwig von Moltke (referred to as "von Moltke the Younger" to differentiate from his uncle that had the same name). Both uncle and nephew militarists had reputations as fearless commanders on the battlefield. By 1910, "von Moltke the Younger" was in the process of mobilizing the German military for war.

World War I Begins and Then German Atrocities

Between 1910 and 1914, there were sporadic terrorist incidents causing escalating tension across Europe. On June 18, 1914, Serbian ultranationalist, Gavrilo Princip, shot and killed Hapsburg Dynasty heir apparent Archduke Franz Ferdinand and wife, Sophie, as they rode in an open car through the streets of Sarajevo in Bosnia—a highly contested area with inhabitants of the Roman Catholic, Eastern Orthodox, and Islamic faiths. Bosnia then, and later during the 1992-1995 Bosnian War, was replete with ethnic violence verging on total anarchy. In 1914, Serbian insurrectionist violence against the Catholic Hapsburgs was met with harsh, murderous reprisals enacted by the fearsome military of the Austro-Hungarian Empire. The June 1914 assassinations of the Archduke and his wife were followed by steep monetary and territorial demands directed at Slavic Serbia. Although Serbia readily acceded to most Austrian demands, long-standing hatreds over culture, ethnicity, language, and religion prevailed. On July 28, 1914, the massive Austro-Hungarian Empire declared war on Serbia. In response, Russian Czar Nicholas II ordered preparations for war against Austria-Hungary. Surprisingly and ironically, arch-militarist *Kaiser* Wilhelm II attempted, at the last hour, to *avert* war. In the night between July 29 and 30, 1914, the German *Kaiser* sent urgent last-ditch telegrams to his Austrian allies to preclude war. Wilhelm II's motivation for making an eleventh-hour attempt to prevent war stemmed from deep-seated fear of the formidable British army and navy. British Foreign Secretary Sir Edward Grey made it abundantly clear to the *Kaiser* that Great Britain would militarily support France and its ally, Russia. With the thought of fighting the entirety of the British Empire, Wilhelm II now had last-minute misgivings. However, it was "too little, too late" to stop the war. Throughout Europe, war and its consequences were becoming a dreaded reality. In England, Sir Grey foresaw doom in a letter to a friend expressing the following lament: "The lamps of Europe are going out all over Europe, we shall not see them lit again in our life-time" (August 3, 1914).

During the 19th century, the Austro-Hungarian Hapsburg rulers were ardent foes of Italy. By the end of the century, however, the Hapsburgs promised to cede territories to Italy, if the southern European country would join its alliance with Germany. With trepidation, Italy agreed to form the "Triple Alliance." However, the Italian diplomats were loath to trust the duplicitous Hapsburgs. Thus, in the prelude to the Great War, the Italians began secret military negotiations with Great Britain and France. As a consequence, Italy withdrew from the Triple Alliance and became a "neutral country" on August 3, 1914. Less than nine months later, on April 26, 1915, Italian Minister of Foreign Affairs, Sidney

Sonnino, signed the Treaty of London and thus joined "*Le Triple Entente*" in war against the Austro-Hungarian Empire. This agreement stipulated that Italy would ally militarily with Great Britain, France, and Russia. In return, these nations pledged that the Italian-speaking regions of the Austro-Hungarian Empire, which included the city of Trentino, the South Tyrol Mountains, and major port city of Trieste, would become part of Italy.

Prior to 1914, Cecil Spring Rice issued repeated warnings concerning the *Kaiser*'s hegemonic ambitions in the conquest of land and power. His alerts proved to be prescient and deadly accurate. By August 1914, the German-led juggernaut through Europe crushed any person or nation that crossed its path. In WWI, the Germans perpetrated what could only be described as "state-sponsored terrorism." The German army invasion into neutral Belgium resulted in the razing of hundreds of villages. The "Huns" (the name used by Wilhelm II for his troops) murdered thousands of civilians in what was labeled "the destruction of poor little Belgium." The Kaiser's naval armada committed mass murder at sea with U-boats (*Unterbooten*) sinking civilian passenger ships and merchant freighters without warning. Germany violated international maritime laws, specifically the "Cruiser Rules," by perpetrating, for the first time in history, widespread "unrestricted submarine warfare." On May 7, 1915, the stately British passenger ship *RMS Lusitania* was torpedoed without warning. The ocean liner sank in 18 minutes and resulted in the deaths of 1,198 passengers and crew--128 of which were Americans. The sinking of passenger ships obviously alarmed the American public. In response, President Wilson issued a strong condemnation to the Germans for their heinous acts at sea. However, the American president steadfastly held to strict U.S. neutrality. Wilson's many isolationist supporters repeatedly espoused the popular pacifist mantra: "He kept us out of war!" In contrast to Wilson's absence of action, former U.S. President Theodore Roosevelt strongly advocated *for* war. In the following magazine article, TR directly accused the Germans of "Murder on the High Seas":

The German submarines have established no effective blockade of the British and French coastlines. They have endeavored to prevent access of French, British *and neutral* ships to Britain and France by attacks upon them which defy every principle of international law as laid down in innumerable existing treaties, including The Hague Convention. Many of these attacks have represented pure piracy; and not a few of them have been accompanied by murder on an extended scale. In the case of the *Lusitania* the scale was so vast that the murder became wholesale. (*Metropolitan Magazine*, May 9, 1915)

America Goes to War

Prior to April 1917, the U.S.A. was officially neutral in the war and could theoretically sell war supplies to any nation. Since the British Navy formed a nautical cordon blocking shipments to Germany and the Central Powers, supplies could only be shipped to the Allies. The British blockade caused widespread famine throughout Germany. The Germans resorted to sabotage on American soil to stem the flow of U.S.A. war materiel to Great Britain and France. Under the clandestine directive of the *Kaiser's* Ambassador to the U.S., Johann Heinrich Graf von Bernstorff, an edgy young Czech immigrant named Michael Kristoff was recruited as a saboteur. Kristoff was ordered to plant delayed-fuse "glass bombs" on barges moored to Black Tom Island—a man-made islet attached by bridge to Jersey City. On July 30, 1916, these bombs ignited munitions stowed in moored ships that created shock waves felt as far away as Philadelphia—90 miles from Black Tom Island. Hundreds were injured from shattered window glass in Jersey City and across lower Manhattan Island. There were an estimated seven fatalities. (The exact number is unknown because bodies disintegrated in the blasts.) Nearby on Bedloe's Island (renamed Liberty Island in 1956), the Statue of Liberty sustained the impact of over a thousand metal shards from the blasts. The metal shards easily punctured the huge, two-penny deep copper-skinned statue, especially Liberty's torch. Henceforth, the torch was--and is still--off-limits to visitors due to the weakening of the structure as a result of the damage sustained in the 1916 blast.

On August 4, 1914, the British cut all German-owned undersea transatlantic cables. The sole remaining undersea cables were owned and operated by the British and the Americans. Thus, the Germans relied on the undersea cables of neutral America to send messages. The U.S. required, however, that these messages not be encoded. The Germans complied, except for the secret message sent by German Foreign Minister Arthur Zimmermann. This secret message was sent to the Mexican government. The British were given access to this encoded cable message. After spending considerable effort in decoding this January 11, 1917 communiqué, British authorities were aghast by its contents. In the communiqué, the Germans offered Mexico vast portions of American territory in return for Mexico declaring war on and attacking the U.S.A. The Zimmermann telegram was exposed to the American public, who were shocked and angered by this German scheme. In response, President Wilson again vehemently protested to the German government.

Drawing showing the intent of the Zimmermann telegram:
Carving out areas of the U.S.A. to be "given"
by the Germans to Mexico
for help in fighting the Americans.

Wilson also pleaded with the German government to cease unrestricted submarine warfare. The Germans complied, but only for a short time. With the British naval blockade cordoning off German ports, mass starvation was spreading throughout Germany. In response to the British blockade, the *Kaiser* decreed that effective on February 1, 1917 there would be a reinstitution of unrestricted submarine warfare. Furthermore, the renewed threat affected even more countries. From that time forward, U-boats would sink ships of *any* nation not allied to the Central Powers. Additionally, Wilhelm II forbad his U-boat crews from attempting rescues of survivors. With this February 1 edict by the *Kaiser*, Wilson protested yet again calling for a cessation of the German's use of unrestricted submarine warfare.

On February 25, 1917, a German U-boat launched two torpedoes into and sank the *RMS Laconia*. Twelve died, including two Americans--Mary Hoy and her daughter Elizabeth. Floyd Gibbons, a writer for the *Chicago Tribune*, was onboard the same torpedoed ship but survived. His emotionally charged dispatches to his newspaper were unnerving. He described in detail how the Hoys, mother and daughter, died. Both were on a damaged, partially submerged life raft. With seawater up to their waists, the American women died a slow, agonizing death from the elements in the frigid Atlantic Ocean. Gibbons' report of the incident shocked and angered the American public, who were utterly disgusted that "American women were being killed by the Germans." As the Hoys were acquaintances of First Lady Edith Bolling Galt Wilson, their deaths had a personal impact on the beleaguered U.S. president. In response, President Wilson sent to Congress what could best be described as a halfway measure between neutrality and war. Titled the "Armed Neutrality Bill of February 26, 1917," the measure would have permitted U.S.-flagged ships to fire on German U-boats. Those in Congress against U.S. intervention in the war raging in Europe were opposed to Wilson's bill on the grounds that he was circuitously bringing the U.S.A. into the war. Those in Congress advocating for intervention deemed the measure as grossly insufficient. With opposition from both sides on this contentious issue, the measure did not come close to passage in Congress.

The next month, March 1917, President Wilson became withdrawn from the public claiming he had a "cold." While this may be true, it is also certain that Wilson was mentally torn between keeping his country out of war or finally entering into war on the side of the Allies. After much emotional duress and soul searching, Wilson reluctantly decided in favor of war. On April 2, 1917, Wilson addressed a joint session of the U.S. Congress and asked that a declaration of war be enacted against the German Imperial Government. The following are portions of Wilson's address to Congress:

> It is a fearful thing to lead this great peaceful people into war, into the most terrible and disastrous of all wars, civilization itself seeming to be in the balance... The world must be made safe for democracy. Its peace must be planted upon the tested foundations of political liberty. We have no selfish ends to serve. We desire no conquest, no dominion. We seek no indemnities for ourselves, no material compensation for the sacrifices we shall freely make.
>
> We are but one of the champions of the rights of mankind. We shall be satisfied when those rights have been made as secure as the faith and the freedom of nations can make them. Just because we fight without rancor and without selfish object, seeking nothing for ourselves but what we shall wish to share with all free peoples, we shall, I feel confident, conduct our operations as belligerents without passion and ourselves observe with proud punctilio the principles of right and of fair play we profess to be fighting for. (President Thomas Woodrow Wilson's address to a joint session of the U.S. Congress made on April 2, 1917.)

Just months earlier, a majority of Americans and those in Congress leaned toward keeping the U.S. a *neutral* nation.

However, by spring 1917 with the Germans escalating atrocities, a majority of Americans across the nation and in Congress shifted towards the U.S. intervening in the war. In his address to Congress, President Woodrow Wilson coined an iconic phrase: "The world must be made safe for democracy." Congress approved Wilson's war bill with just a handful of "nay" votes on April 6, 1917. Eight months later, on December 7, 1917, the U.S. declared war on the Austro-Hungarian Empire. In a note of irony, 24 years later on this day, the U.S. was attacked at its Hawaiian Naval and Army facilities at Pearl Harbor by Imperial Japan. This December 7, 1941 attack thrust the U.S.A. into World War II.

TR and Spring Rice in WWI

Acknowledging Spring Rice's affinity for the Americans, government authorities in Whitehall (London) appointed him British Ambassador to the United States. The ambassadorial appointment was made in 1912. However, Spring Rice could not travel overseas due to a debilitating bout of erysipelas skin disease. Thus, his posting in America was delayed until 1913 (Burton, 1999, p. 64). When he finally arrived in the U.S.A., Sir Spring Rice sported a beard to hide the remnant scars from erysipelas. Burton (1990) comments about Spring Rice: "He came to Washington, D.C. in April 1913, intent on representing his country in the best way possible, which for him was promoting Anglo-American understanding" (p. 43). In Washington, D.C., the British Ambassador began a seemingly endless series of meetings with American politicians and foreign diplomats. Spring Rice conferred with his French counterpart, who offered some important advice. French Ambassador to the U.S. Jean Jules Adrien Jusserand cautioned Spring Rice to not overtly fraternize with the Republicans—especially TR, who was Woodrow Wilson's opponent in the 1912 presidential election. Historian Edward J. Renehan (1998) also commented on the warning given to Spring Rice: "…He was advised by his [the British] government to avoid TR at all costs for fear of alienating Woodrow Wilson, with whom he had to do business" (p. 120).

Performing cautiously and diligently as British Ambassador, Spring Rice maintained cordial relations with cabinet members of the Wilson Administration and leaders of the Democratic Party. Privately, however, the British Ambassador corresponded and met with key Republicans such as Henry Adams, John Hay, Henry Cabot Lodge, and, of course, Theodore Roosevelt. In April 1913, Spring Rice wrote to his longtime New York friend lamenting: "Oh, T.R., how I wish I could see you. I nearly wept at Rock Creek" [a Washington, D.C. nature reserve where the Briton and TR strolled at an earlier time while discussing international events] (Renehan, p. 120). Wilson was an astute politician, who was fully aware of the close friendship between Sir Spring Rice and TR. Thus, Wilson kept a skeptical eye on the British Ambassador. However, with Europe engulfed in total war, Wilson could not afford to ignore for long Spring Rice and his prescient warnings regarding German territorial ambitions.

By 1914, TR had become an archly conservative voice regarding international affairs. Virtually on a daily basis, TR delivered patriotic--some would view as xenophobic--speeches across the U.S.A. He also wrote scores of magazine and newspaper articles stressing military preparedness and nationalism. In fact, a consistent theme in his orations and writings was "unambiguous nationalism." In the fall of 1915, TR exhorted on this topic and also upon what he deemed to be a "good American":

> There is no room in this country for hyphenated Americanism. When I refer to hyphenated Americans, I do not refer to naturalized Americans. Some of the very best Americans I have ever known were naturalized Americans, Americans born abroad. But a hyphenated American is not an American at all... There is no such thing as a hyphenated American who is a good American. The only man who is a good American is the man who is an American and nothing else. (Excerpt from a speech to the mainly Irish Catholic Knights of Columbus "Grand Assembly" at Carnegie Hall, Columbus Day, October 12, 1915.)

Theodore Roosevelt delivering
an always energetic and ferociously gestured
speech usually with one or more clenched fists.

Unlike Spring Rice, who always acted and spoke diplomatically, TR had no such inhibitions. Repeatedly in speeches and in published articles, TR lambasted the Wilson Administration. He called President Wilson "the chief spokesperson for the 'flub-dubs,' 'mollycoddles,' and 'flap-doodle pacifists' who were too yellow to fight" (Renehan, p. 121). TR wrote to his British friend wildly boasting that "…had he been president, he would have stepped in and saved Belgium from being overrun" (Renehan, p. 121). Though lifelong friends with Spring Rice, TR was temperamentally quite different. TR thirsted for bloodlust. In at least three continents, TR shot hundreds of animals that became his hunting trophies. His Sagamore Hill home displays dozens of animal heads. TR also shot and killed one or more Spaniards at close range in the Spanish American War. The "exuberant" former U.S. president was often seen with clenched fists. TR was more than eager to deliver jabs and punches to *desperados*–this time not the Dakota Badlands cattle thieves, but the ruthless "Huns" overrunning

Europe. The following photograph with super-imposed wording is self-explanatory.

Photograph of Theodore Roosevelt with a
quite obvious sentiment superimposed: "The Fists of TR."

On the other hand, his British friend, Sir Spring Rice, was gentile and diplomatic—both by profession and by temperament. In the following letter, Spring Rice expressed his worries concerning the German threat, while at the same time addressing his nation's moral fiber in terms of freedom, justice, and truth:

> I am not much in favor of asking for sympathy. We shall stand or fall by what we do, by and what others do, and not by what other people think; and I don't like fierce efforts to convince Americans that we are in the right. The question is: 'Is freedom strong enough to defend itself?' A government is either too strong for the freedom of its own people, or too weak to defend them from a foreign enemy. We choose the last form. However, if there is justice or truth in the world, we shall win in the end; and if there is no justice or truth, it isn't worth living here—so we can leave it at that. (Personal correspondence to Professor H. E. Luxmoore, Tutor at Eton College, dated September 24, 1914.)

Photograph of Sir Cecil Spring Rice,
British Ambassador to the U.S.
(1913-1918).

Shortly after the U.S. declared war on Germany in April 1917, TR telegraphed President Wilson requesting permission to organize a volunteer regiment, akin to his two decade earlier Rough Riders. In Wilson's telegraph reply, the American president declined TR's offer due to the fact that warfare had drastically evolved into highly mechanized carnage replete with huge "no-man's-land" killing fields between muddy, disease-ridden trenches. This type of warfare was far removed from TR's experiences in the Spanish American War. Since then, there were warplanes, tanks, and deadly poison gas. Wilson made clear in his telegraphed denial to TR that his decision was not personal. Whether or not this was true, it was obvious that TR was not physically fit to command troops on the battlefield. Now at age 58, TR was blind in one eye, had an ashen pallor, and had much difficulty walking due to leg abscesses. In fact, these leg ulcers and other medical ailments would end TR's life in less than two years.

Spring Rice was also in waning health with his Graves' (thyroid) disease a major concern. After making public appearances and speech making across America on behalf of the WWI Allies, Cecil

Spring Rice and TR were becoming exhausted. However, neither Spring Rice nor TR would slow down, let alone stop, any of their efforts. They perceived their tireless exertions as a symbol of patriotism for their beloved countries.

<u>Causes and Aftermath of WWI</u>

The assassinations of Archduke Ferdinand and his wife are often deemed the cause of the Great War. While this incident sparked the conflict, it was other factors that engulfed Europe in bloodshed. The most salient cause for the war was the decision made by *Kaiser* Wilhelm II to conquer Belgium and invade France. To the German people the Teutonic Caesar was also their "Supreme War Lord." The *Kaiser* decreed a "New Course" for Germany that included not only murderous invasions of its neighboring countries but also unrestricted submarine warfare and the widespread indiscriminate use of poison gas as weapons of terror. Wilhelm II reminded his imperial army troops that they were the offspring of the millennium earlier "Attila and his Huns." In August 1914, the latter day Huns invaded and quickly seized control of lightly defended Belgium. The Germans were brutal and bloodthirsty. In responding to trumped-up charges of attacks on German troops, these 20th century Huns perpetrated reprisals that resulted in the murder of 6,427 innocent Belgian civilians. The *Kaiser* next ordered the invasion of northeastern France. With the invasions of Belgium and France, Germany forced Great Britain into the war. This conflict resulted in 36.5 million casualties and was grossly mislabeled "The War to End All Wars." WWI stretched over six continents and continued until the eleventh hour of the eleventh day in 1918, when an armistice stopped—for only twenty-one years--the fighting, the destruction, and the human misery of warfare.

After the First World War, the autocratic empires of Germany, Austria-Hungary, the Ottomans, and Russia came to ignominious ends. Germany lost its colonial outposts in Africa and Asia. Much of its industrial infrastructure was damaged in the war. For this, Germany experienced hyperinflation and turmoil. The

Austro-Hungarian Empire was split apart. Austria and Hungary became separate countries. Much of the remaining territory of the Hapsburg's realm became Yugoslavia. After the death of the Yugoslavian dictator Marshall Josip Broz Tito in 1980, Yugoslavia itself splintered into separate, warring nations. Warfare has flared among these Balkan nations based on deep-seated ethnic and religious hatreds. Similarly, the Ottoman Empire ended with the establishment of the Republic of Turkey and other, mostly Islamic, Middle East nations. As with the Balkans, civil war and terrorism in the Middle East has persisted to the present day. The rule of the Romanovs in Russia ended with the wholesale murder of the centuries-old noble family. Taking the place of the Romanovs were the brutal Bolsheviks and later the territorially aggressive and fierce Marxist Communists.

Before World War I, the British could boast that: "The Sun never sets on the British Empire." Following the war, the British were compelled by bloodshed and principle to cede 83.5 percent of the island called Eire to the independent Republic of Ireland. Many other component countries of the British Empire yearned for independence. The British people were wise and ennobled to respond after the war by forming the invaluable, devolved British Commonwealth of Nations in 1921. The U.S.A. did not enter the war for territorial gains. Rather, the Americans intervened to stop the murderous *Kaiser* and his modern day "Huns." The U.S.A. came out of the Great War strengthened as a global economic and military power, but still flawed with overt racism. African American "Doughboys" returning from France faced in their own country abject discrimination and infamous "Black Codes" and "Jim Crow laws."

Certainly the greatest sin of the First World War combatant nations was their inability to prevent the Second World War from occurring. These nations strenuously tried but failed with the "League of Nations." Since the WWI armistice only stopped the fighting, peace was not to last. From 1939 until 1945, the world was again at war. WWI would cause immense suffering. However, WWII was far worse in all respects—especially in the number of civilian casualties. *Hopefully there will never be a World War III!*

Posthumous Honors for Theodore Roosevelt

This essay has focused on Theodore Roosevelt and Sir Cecil Spring Rice in World War I. With the 1918 armistice, the fighting ceased. During that year, "Springy," one of TR's closest friends, died on February 14, 1918. TR also had to face the death of his son, Quentin, who was killed in aerial combat over France on July 14, 1918. That year, TR's three other sons—Theodore, Jr., Kermit, and Archibald--were all infantry officers recuperating from wounds sustained in the war. Worst injured was Archibald "Archie" Roosevelt, who was "totally disabled" from wounds in his left arm and leg. During 1918, formerly robust Theodore Roosevelt was ailing as well. His worst health problems stemmed from injuries from multiple accidents and an attempted assassination. In 1902, TR and wife, Edith, were injured, and a federal agent was killed, when a trolley car crashed into their open landau. William Craig, assigned to protect TR, was the first U.S. Secret Agent killed while serving in the line of duty. TR suffered from asthma all his life. To cope with this malady, TR lifted weights and boxed from his boyhood to his later life. In 1908, the 50-year old U.S. president's left eye was bloodied while he sparred with a professional boxer in the White House. The damage to his eye resulted in permanent partial blindness. In October 1912, TR was nearly assassinated just before delivering a campaign speech in Milwaukee. He was shot in the chest at point blank range. Although weak, and with his clothes spattered with blood, the stalwart New Yorker refused to go to the hospital before he delivered his speech. Only after he made his two-hour long speech did TR agree to medical treatment. Fortunately, the 32-caliber bullet shot by the would-be assassin had to pass through a fifty-page text of TR's speech and was deflected by a metal eyeglass case stuffed in his chest pocket. However, his best armament was his highly muscled tree-trunk barreled chest!

Even so, doctors feared the bullet, so close to his heart, could not be safely removed. So there it stayed for the rest of Roosevelt's life.

The battered former U.S. president suffered from bouts of malarial fever as well as ear infections. He also had leg ulcerations stemming from the 1902 cable car accident that were acerbated during the 1913-1914 Amazon River expedition. These leg injuries never entirely healed. During the last weeks of 1918, TR became weak with a throat virus and a very high fever. Thus, he was brought to Roosevelt Hospital—an institution that was funded by TR's distant cousin James Henry Roosevelt in 1863. His breathing was labored and loud. In the first days of 1919, TR's fever temperature subsided and he was cautiously released from the hospital. Nevertheless, in the early hours of January 6, 1919, the 60-year old former U.S. president suffered a pulmonary embolism and died of heart failure while asleep at his Sagamore Hill, Long Island, home. [Note: Following a three-year, $8.5 million restoration, the immensely popular Sagamore Hill National Historic Site of the U.S. National Park Service was most thankfully re-opened on July 12, 2015.]

TR would receive numerous honors during his lifetime, including the Nobel Peace Prize for brokering a peace treaty between the warring nations of the Russo-Japanese War (1905). However, for 103 years, the U.S. Army was intransigent in denying him the U.S. Congressional Medal of Honor for his leadership and valor in the Spanish American War. This denial can be traced to TR's public criticism of the U.S. War Department for its long delay in bringing his Rough Riders regiment home from Cuba in 1898. The oversight of TR not receiving the U.S. Congressional Medal of Honor was remedied on January 16, 2001. That day, Roosevelt was posthumously awarded the U.S. nation's highest honor. At a White House ceremony, televised and archived by C-SPAN, President Bill Clinton remarked: "Sometimes it takes this country awhile, but we nearly always get to correct what is a significant historical error--in this case denying TR the 'Medal of Honor.'" Tweed

Roosevelt—a bespectacled visage of TR sans the mustache and huge teeth—accepted the award on behalf of his great-grandfather. The following is TR's "Medal of Honor" citation:

> For conspicuous gallantry and intrepidity at the risk of his life above and beyond the call of duty, Lieutenant Colonel Theodore Roosevelt distinguished himself by acts of bravery on 1 July 1898 while leading a daring charge up San Juan Hill. Lieutenant Colonel Roosevelt, in total disregard for his personal safety, led a desperate and gallant charge up San Juan Hill, encouraging his troops to continue the assault through withering enemy fire over open countryside. Facing the enemy's heavy fire, he displayed extraordinary bravery throughout the charge, and was the first to reach the enemy trenches, where he killed one of the enemy with his pistol, allowing his men to continue the assault. His leadership and valor turned the tide in the Battle of San Juan Hill. His extraordinary heroism and devotion to duty are in keeping with the highest traditions of military service and reflect great credit upon himself, his unit, and the United States Army. (http://www.c-span.org/video/?161885-1/medal-honor-ceremony; Retrieved 2/29/2016).

American artist Frederick Sackrider Remington's painting of Lt. Colonel Roosevelt bravely leading the charge up San Juan Hill, Cuba, 1898.

One of the last photographs of TR
as he cuddles his granddaughter just a short
time before he died on January 6, 1919.

The New York Times (January 7, 1919)
front page that includes a lengthy obituary
of Theodore Roosevelt, who died in his sleep
the previous day.

Sir Cecil Spring Rice Posthumously Recognized

Upon his appointment as Ambassador to the U.S., Spring Rice's underlying mission was to encourage the Americans to abandon neutrality and join forces with the Allies. When the U.S. entered WWI in April 1917, the British government deemed Spring Rice's mission to be fulfilled and thus at an end. With his task completed, Foreign Office authorities in London repeatedly requested that Spring Rice return to England. He stubbornly refused to vacate his ambassadorship in Washington, D.C. He asserted that his continued presence in the U.S.A. was of vital importance. British King George V then intervened. At the beginning of 1918, the British King personally requested that he return home. The monarch offered an additional, justly earned, reason for Spring Rice's return. King George V was going to bestow upon him the peerage title "Lord Spring Rice." The British diplomat finally agreed to return to England. D. H. Burton (1990) writes: "In his own mind it was certain that he [Spring Rice] succeeded, at great personal cost, by driving himself relentlessly" (p. 44). In early February 1918, undoubtedly worn out from his extended labors in Washington, D.C., the British ambassador began his journey home to England via Canada. Spring Rice died in Ottawa on February 14, 1918, 13 days shy of his 59th birthday. To the world press, Sir Spring Rice's death was listed as "unexpected." However, the British Ambassador was ill and completely exhausted by the time he left the American capital. Shortly before leaving Washington, D.C., he revised an earlier poem, "*Urbs Dei*," with a new first verse and title. Spring Rice sent copies of "I Vow to Thee, My Country" to those he loved and respected.

Sir Cecil Arthur Spring Rice was bestowed with many honors during his lifetime including: "Knight Grand Cross of the Order of St. Michael and St. George" (GCMG; 1906) and "Knight Grand Cross of the Royal Victorian Order" (GCVO; 1908). In 1913, he was also made a member of the British Royal Privy Council (PC) and Court of the Star Chamber. Shortly after he died in 1918, the mountain range that serves as the partial border between the Canadian Provinces of Alberta and British Columbia was renamed Mount Spring-Rice (here his double surname is hyphenated). In 1919, Lord Robert Cecil, a founder of the League of Nations and a recipient of the Nobel Peace Prize, spoke glowingly of Spring Rice's pivotal role in encouraging the U.S.A. to join the Allies in WWI and for fostering the bond between Great Britain and America. In addressing the British House of Commons, Lord Cecil firmly asserted: "No ambassador has ever had to discharge duties of greater delicacy or of more far reaching importance than fell to his lot. Nor has any ambassador ever fulfilled this task with more unwearied vigilance, conspicuous ability, and ultimate success" (Gwynn, 1929, p. 436).

British Foreign Minister Arthur James Balfour, 1st earl of Balfour, said Cecil Spring Rice was "An ambassador who has never spared himself." British author, historian, and journalist Sir Ignatius Valentine Chirol penned an apt and touching "In Memoriam" commending Sir Spring Rice. Chirol was deeply appreciative of the British Ambassador's selfless service especially during his final years while he suffered from ill health:

> The lines [of "I Vow to Thee, My Country"] were written by Sir Cecil Arthur Spring-Rice, His Majesty's Ambassador to the United States, on the eve of his final departure from Washington. The vow recorded in this poem had been kept long before he put it into words, for he had served his country for a quarter of a century with the "love that never falters"; and though he did not know it, he was already a dying man. With his singular clarity of vision, he had realized at the beginning of the war that its issue might well depend on the last resort on the attitude of the great American Republic; and so acute a sense as his of the awful responsibility that rested in such circumstances upon a British Ambassador during the prolonged period of American hesitation and neutrality, would have told severely on a much more robust constitution. If diplomacy may be compared to active warfare, he had fought for two years in the most dangerous and important salient of the British lines... (http://babel.hathitrust.org/cgi/pt?id=coo1.ark:/13960/t6g16k11c;view=1up;seq=9; Retrieved 2/29/2016).

D. H. Burton (1999) sums up the British Ambassador's unmatched legacy: "Spring Rice was thoroughly pro-American without ever losing sight of his responsibility to his own government" (p. 63). In recent years, however, Cecil A. Spring Rice's achievements have been somewhat "buried in history" according to the former British Deputy Consul to Canada, Honourable Ashley Prime. His knowledge of Spring Rice's accomplishments occurred indirectly as he searched the Internet for the author of the inspiring words of *I Vow to Thee, My Country*, a poignant hymn that was played at his father's funeral in 1983. Prime discovered that Spring Rice wrote the words to an iconic poem that was in 1921 set to the music of British-born composer Gustav Holst. Both Spring Rice and Prime were alumni of Balliol College. The former Deputy Consul to Canada was further impressed with Spring Rice's tireless diplomatic efforts in attaining U.S. support for the Allies during the Great War. The present day British diplomat has led an effort in raising a new—highly justified--awareness of Spring Rice's many accomplishments.

Former Deputy Consul to
Canada Honourable Ashley Prime.

On June 7, 2013, a bronze plaque was unveiled at the gravesite of Sir Cecil Spring Rice, resting amidst the meticulously landscaped Beechwood, The National Cemetery of Canada, located south of Ottawa. At the gravesite ceremony, Ms. Caroline Kenny, a retired primary schoolteacher who lives in Sussex, England, warmly thanked those individuals who have rekindled the appreciation of her grandfather's many achievements.

June 7, 2013 photograph of Honourable Ashley Prime speaking with Ms. Caroline Kenny in front of the grave of her grandfather, Cecil Arthur Spring Rice, at Beechwood, The National Cemetery of Canada at an unveiling ceremony for a bronze plaque.

At the ceremony, a commemorative plaque was unveiled featuring an excerpt from Sir Cecil Arthur Spring Rice's patriotic and poignant poem: "I Vow to Thee, My Country." At this highly poignant event, Ms. Kelly Sloan sang the widely beloved patriotic Cecil Spring Rice/Gustav Holst hymn *I Vow to Thee, My Country*.

Acknowledgement: Ms. Nicole Bedard, Development Coordinator of Beechwood, The National Cemetery of Canada, provided access to essential source material and photographs used in this essay. Thanks also to the British and Canadian government authorities for their assistance.

Sir Spring Rice's "I Vow to Thee, My Country"

The WWI armistice took effect on the eleventh hour of the eleventh day of 1918. By this time, there were 16.5 million dead and 20 million wounded (http://ww1facts.net/quick-reference/ww1-casualties/; Retrieved 2/29/2016). Included in this carnage was the ambassador's brother, Gerald Spring Rice, who perished in 1916 on the Western Front in France. In the century following World War I, the Commonwealth of Nations commemorates "Remembrance

Day." The United Kingdom does not have an official national anthem, though *God Save the Queen* very often serves in this function. In a recent poll to determine what hymn or melody should be an official UK national anthem, *I Vow to Thee, My Country* "was placed third amongst the contenders" (http://anthem4england.co.uk/anthems/i-vow-to-thee-my-country/; Retrieved 2/29/2016).

It is most likely that no hymn, however poignant and grand, will ever replace *God Save the Queen* as an official national anthem. Yet, the words of Cecil Spring Rice, combined with the majestic, highly melodic music of Gustav Holst, form a patriotic masterpiece that is genuinely cherished throughout the United Kingdom and the Commonwealth of Nations. The origin of the musical collaboration also bears description. British composer Ralph Vaughn Williams was the first artist approached to set Spring Rice's poem to music. Vaughn Williams delegated this task to his close friend, Gustav Holst, who was an expert in resurrecting old English folk tunes to enlighten modern audiences. However, in this case, Holst used the main section of his orchestral suite *The Planets—Jupiter, the Bringer of Jollity*, for this purpose. Holst's musical adaptation was completed in 1921. The hymn is beloved by many, but not everyone. Some in the religious community criticize the Spring Rice/Holst hymn for putting "country" in the first verse and "God" in the second verse. Critics of the hymn represent a small minority, because it is widely performed at many official ceremonies. These events have included the 1965 funeral of Sir Winston Churchill. The late Princess Diana Spencer revered this hymn from her early school years and had it played at her July 29, 1981 wedding; and, sadly, it was performed again at her 1997 funeral. On May 21, 1988, Prime Minister Margaret Thatcher ended her notable address to the General Assembly of the Church of Scotland by excerpting portions of Spring Rice's poem. The 2005 funeral of one of Canada's most highly decorated WWII heroes, Sergeant Ernest "Smokey" Smith, included the Spring Rice/Holst hymn. The hymn—with repeated stanzas--was sung with organ accompaniment throughout the lengthy procession of placing poppies on Sergeant Smith's coffin. The hymn was performed at Queen Elizabeth II's "60-Year Diamond Jubilee" celebrations in 2012 and at that year's opening ceremonies of the London Paralympics Games. The hymn was performed at the 2013 funeral of Baroness Thatcher—an individual who cherished Spring Rice's poem. The underlying meaning of the Spring Rice/Holst hymn is readily understood and enduringly appropriate for "Remembrance Day" ceremonies throughout the Commonwealth of Nations. In respect to those lost in WWI, and implicitly in all wars, Sir Cecil Arthur Spring Rice composed in early 1918:

I vow to thee my country, all earthly things above.
Entire and whole and perfect, the service of my love;
The love that asks no question, the love that stands the test,
That lays upon the altar the dearest and the best.
The love that never falters, the love that pays the price,
The love that makes undaunted the final sacrifice.

And there's another country, I've heard of long ago,
Most dear to them that love her, most great to them that know.
We may not count her armies; we may not see her King,
Her fortress is a faithful heart, her pride is suffering.
And soul by soul and silently her shining bounds increase,
And her ways are ways of gentleness, and all her paths are peace.

Theodore Roosevelt's Exceptional Family

This essay concludes with descriptions of Theodore Roosevelt's family. The word "exceptional" is overused, but not in the case of TR's family.

TR's Father: Theodore "Thee" Roosevelt, Sr.

The ancestors of TR's father, Theodore "Thee" Roosevelt, Sr., were Dutch settlers in the *Nieuw Nederland* colony that later became New York State. The Dutch influence, then and now, remains an integral component of New York history. This is especially true in *Nieuw Amsterdam,* which eventually became New York City (spelled with a hyphen prior to 1898). Early 19th century American author and satirist Washington Irving referred to these Dutch settlers as "Knickerbockers" as a humorous tease to their rolled-up, ballooned-knee pants called "knickers." In the November 11, 1807 edition of *Salmagundi,* Irving wrote an article that poked fun at New-York City's "Knickerbockers" (Burrows & Wallace, 1999, p. 417). In Irving's 1809 tongue-in-cheek satire: *A History of New-York from the Beginning of the World to the End of Dutch Dynasty*, the widely read author made many references to a fictitious N-YC character bearing common Dutch first and last names: "Dietrich Knickerbocker." Throughout the 19th century and the first half of the 20th century, "Father Knickerbocker" was a widely used, though unofficial, symbol for the city. Beginning in the 1960s, NYC used the somewhat inane phrase and song: "I Love New York." Yet, Dutch names have and are still being used for a wide variety of NYC thoroughfares such as "Flushing" and "Onderdonk" Avenues. The Bronx is named after the Dutchman Jonas Bronck. The extreme southwestern edge of The Bronx is called *Spuyten Duyvil* (Dutch for "Spitting Devil") and the waterway that separates The Bronx from Manhattan is called *Spuyten Duyvil Creek.* "Roosevelt" is a Dutch name that translates into English as "Rose Field."

"Thee" Roosevelt helped "Teedy" (TR's childhood nickname) overcome the near-death ravages of bronchial asthma. During the American Civil War, Georgia-raised Martha "Mittie" Roosevelt deplored having her husband fight against Southerners. Thus, in assenting to his wife's wishes, "Thee" paid for a substitute to fight in the Union Army. While not serving in uniform, "Thee" contributed by donating repeated and substantial sums of money to aid the welfare of returning Union Army soldiers. "Thee" was also very perceptive in immediately detecting the brilliant, inquisitive mind of his son. "Thee" Roosevelt wisely advised TR to build up his body as well as his already burgeoning intellect. TR's father encouraged his son's interests in the natural sciences, including botany, biology, zoology, and taxidermy. While TR was a

Harvard University undergraduate, "Thee" became gravely ill with stomach cancer. Upon notification of his father's failing health, TR immediately left Cambridge, Massachusetts, for home. Alas, "Thee" died several hours before TR reached New-York City on February 9, 1878. Theodore "Thee" Roosevelt was only 46 years old when he died. TR often recalled that the man he admired most in his life was his father.

Photograph of Theodore "Thee" Roosevelt, Sr., shortly before he died at age 46.

TR's Mother: Martha Stewart "Mittie" Bulloch

TR's mother, Martha Stewart "Mittie" Bulloch, was born in Connecticut. When she was four years old, her family moved to Roswell, Georgia. Decades later, "Mittie" Bulloch's bridesmaid and closest friend Evelyn King was interviewed by author Margaret Mitchell. The American novelist was at that time writing an article for the *Atlanta Journal* newspaper seeking to describe the archtype "Southern Belle." Evelyn King described to Mitchell her friend Martha "Mittie" Bulloch as the ideal embodiment of the "Southern Belle." "Mittie" was indeed charming, comely, and, in certain ways, frivolous. Georgia-raised, she spoke with a delicately silken "Southern drawl." As such, TR's mother served to some degree as an exemplar for "Scarlett O'Hara," the main character of Mitchell's 1939 iconic, epic novel: *Gone with the Wind*. In the early morning of February 14, 1884, TR's mother, Martha "Mittie" Bulloch Roosevelt, became gravely ill and died of typhoid fever.

Martha Stewart "Mittie"
Bulloch at age 22.

Alice Hathaway Lee Roosevelt and Alice Lee Roosevelt Longworth

TR was married twice. His first wife, Alice Hathaway Lee Roosevelt, died two days after giving birth to daughter, Alice Lee Roosevelt. Harvard University undergraduate, nineteen-year old TR fell madly in love with and quickly determined he would marry blue-eyed, blond-haired Alice Hathaway Lee, at that point only 17 years of age. At their first encounter, on October 18, 1878, TR wrote in his diary: "As long as I live, I shall never forget how sweetly she looked and how prettily she greeted me." Alice was born on July 19, 1861, and lived in Chestnut Hill, a suburb just west of Brookline, Massachusetts. On June 30, 1880, the future U.S. President graduated from Harvard magna cum laude. Less than four months later on October 27, 1880, Alice and Theodore wed on TR's 22nd birthday. Alice gave birth on February 12, 1884 to a baby girl who bore her name. Two days later, tragedy struck twice.

Alice Hathaway Lee Roosevelt (1861-1884).

TR's mother, Martha Stewart Bulloch Roosevelt, died on the morning of February 14, 1884. Incredibly, on the afternoon of that same day, TR's wife, Alice Hathaway Lee Roosevelt, succumbed to Bright's disease, a kidney ailment that had not been diagnosed as it was masked by pregnancy. Author Nathan Miller (1992) poignantly describes that dreadful day in February 1884 when both TR's mother and wife died:

> Someone murmured that if he wished to see his mother before she died, he should hurry down to her room on the second floor. In the stillness of the morning, he stood with his sisters and brother at her bedside in the same room in which their father had died [six years earlier], and he echoed Elliott's words. 'There is a curse on this house!' Mittie died at 3:00 a.m., and Roosevelt returned to Alice's room in a daze to take her in his arms again. The vigil continued through the

long night and into the following afternoon, when Alice died. It was St. Valentine's Day—the fourth anniversary of their engagement. She was twenty-two years old. (p. 156)

TR was understandably distraught with the nearly simultaneous deaths of his mother and wife. TR was deeply burdened, perhaps by guilt feelings, for being well over 100 miles away at the Albany legislature and not where his family needed him. Though he wore a positive façade, TR masked—only to a limited degree—his inner turmoil in dealing with this double tragedy. As a sign of depression avoidance, Roosevelt refused to discuss or even mention his first wife to his daughter, Alice—much to the distress of this sensitive, impressionable child. David McCullough (1984) writes: "Of his mother Theodore was to say comparatively little...Of Alice Lee [TR's first wife], Theodore was to say nothing. Nor, supposedly, was her name ever spoken within the new family he and Edith established" (p. 365). Biographer Kathleen Dalton (2002) similarly comments upon Roosevelt's inner anguish and remorse asserting: "His deadened emotions made him write dramatically in his diary: 'For joy or for sorrow my life has now been lived out.' He comforted himself with action and grasped hastily to recreate the life he and Alice had imagined" (p. 90-91). Daughter Alice Lee was also greatly affected by the death of her mother. Author Henry William Brands (1987) describes the moodier side to Alice Lee Roosevelt stating that she was silent as the first Alice's "tomb on the subject." Young Alice described her mother as being "charming and frivolous and rather hideously Dickensian... I don't think I would have liked my mother very much" (p. 381). Daughter Alice Lee Roosevelt exhibited a complex, difficult, and, at times, blatantly rude pattern of behavior throughout her very long life. Deriding established conformity, she displayed a pronounced streak of *cheekiness* whenever she could. Whether her wildness was a form of rebellion is indeterminable. She would probably be labeled, using current vernacular, as *high maintenance*. Alice emulated her irascible father with her abundant stubbornness—a personality trait TR possessed in abundance!

Alice Lee Roosevelt Longworth
(1884-1980).

Alice Lee Roosevelt's high-spiritedness is clearly evident—even if in jest—within TR's witticism. While serving as U.S. president, TR responded to White House reporters who were questioning Alice Lee's wild behavior. The exasperated Commander-in-Chief asserted that he was able to fulfill his country's chief executive responsibilities or he could control Alice Lee, but he could not do both! Alice led a life replete with social flair and much notoriety, especially after her high-profile February 17, 1906 marriage to Speaker of the U.S. House of Representatives Nicholas "Nick" Longworth III (1869-1931). Forever witty, outspoken, and irreverent, Alice Lee had a favorite pillow fittingly embroidered: "If you can't say something nice about someone, then sit next to me!" In the early 1960s, Alice Lee, then in her mid-70s, assisted First Lady Jacqueline Kennedy in a major White House restoration project. Though Alice Lee Roosevelt Longworth was the first borne of TR's children, she outlived all her siblings, passing away at the age of 96 on February 20, 1980.

Indomitable Wife: Edith Kermit Carow Roosevelt

TR has been labeled in literature and documentary film as "indomitable." Considering Edith Kermit Carow was married to the unrelenting dynamo called Theodore Roosevelt for over 32 years, "indomitable" could also be applied to her. Daughter of New-York City residents Charles Carow and Gertrude Elizabeth Tyler Carow, Edith was born on August 6, 1861. In her childhood, Edith spent much time with TR's younger sister Corinne. According to the Theodore Roosevelt Association website, TR's mother invited "Edie" (as she was called) to join the younger Roosevelt children for her earliest schooling. This took place at the Roosevelt home and included Theodore's Aunt Anna, who was also the Roosevelt children's governess. Soon, Edith became a constant companion to TR at outings, especially—and presciently—in Oyster Bay, NY. Poignantly, it was Edith that TR painted on the transom of his little rowboat the summer he was 16 and she a mere 13. His family expected them to marry, but the summer of 1878 was a turning point in their relationship. It was then as a result of volatile temperaments--especially TR's--that their relationship ended. Though reluctant to marry after the devastating loss of his first wife, TR had a *change of heart* some years after Alice's death when he secretly resumed a close relationship with Edith in 1885. TR and Edith were married in London on December 2, 1886. The couple settled down in the house originally intended for Alice Hathaway Lee at Sagamore Hill. The house was abuzz with Roosevelt children, relatives, and neighbors. As the Theodore Roosevelt Association website asserts, Sagamore Hill became the bustling *headquarters* for a quickly growing family. Edith and TR had five children together: Theodore, Jr., Kermit, Ethel, Archibald and Quentin. When TR became president, Edith assumed the vital role of "First Lady." She was also occupied, to say the least, with being the stepmother to rebellious Alice and the mother to *six* additional children. Though she had five children biologically, Edith claimed TR as her sixth child!

The White House social calendar, with Edith in charge, was a vibrant, thriving center of activities. Her White House concerts, or *musicales* as she called them, were the first to feature musical performances on such a grand scale. Edith is described as cultured, dignified, and scholarly, with a keen wit and a love of poetry. According to the Theodore Roosevelt Association website, under Edith's careful eye, the White House collections of china and the portraits of First Ladies were begun. Edith played a major role in the largest renovation of White House interior décor up to that point in time. Considering TR's job title, President of the United States of America, it is interesting to note that Edith was considered a better judge of *men and money*. A famous TR quote is: "Keep your eyes on the stars but your feet firmly planted on the ground!" Regarding the Roosevelt household, TR's expansive mind was on achievement, honor, and adventure, that is, "the stars." On the other hand, Edith's mind was on the efficient running of the White House. Thus, one may say that her "feet were firmly planted on the ground."

First Lady Edith Kermit Carow Roosevelt
(1861-1948).

After TR's death in 1919, Edith traveled extensively, including visits to Puerto Rico in 1929 when her eldest son, TR, Jr., served as Governor. Shortly thereafter, Edith visited her son in The Philippines, where he was serving as Governor General. Edith bravely endured the tragic war deaths of three sons—Quentin in

1918, Kermit in 1943, and TR, Jr., in 1944. Reaching the age of 87, she passed away on September 30, 1948. Edith was buried beside her dearest Theodore in Youngs Memorial Cemetery, a short distance to the west from their Sagamore Hill home.

Brig. General Theodore "Ted" Roosevelt, Jr., Heroism at Many Levels

Born on November 13, 1887, Ted was the youngest American regimental commander seeing combat and was seriously wounded in World War I. Shortly after returning from war-torn Europe in 1919, Ted was asked by U.S. Army Chief of Staff General John Joseph Pershing to organize a group to honor returning war veterans. TR, Jr. helped establish The American Legion, which was approved by the U.S. Congress on September 16, 1919. *The American Legion's Post Officers Guide* recounts Ted's role in establishing this organization:

> A group of twenty officers who served in the American Expeditionary Forces (A.E.F.) in France in World War I is credited with planning the Legion. A.E.F. Headquarters asked these officers to suggest ideas on how to improve troop morale. One officer, Lieutenant Colonel Theodore Roosevelt, Jr., proposed an organization of veterans. In February 1919, this group formed a temporary committee and selected several hundred officers who had the confidence and respect of the whole army. When the first organization meeting took place in Paris in March 1919, about 1,000 officers and enlisted men attended. The meeting, known as the Paris Caucus, adopted a temporary constitution and the name, The American Legion. It also elected an executive committee to complete the organization's work. It considered each soldier of the A.E.F. a member of the Legion. The executive committee named a subcommittee to organize veterans at home in the U.S. The Legion held a second organizing caucus in St. Louis, Missouri, in May 1919. It completed the constitution and made plans for a permanent organization. It set up temporary headquarters

in New York City, and began its relief, employment, and Americanism programs. Congress granted the Legion a national charter in September 1919. (p. 68)

Amidst the swirl of American Legion activities, Ted Roosevelt found time in 1920 to visit the New York State School Of Applied Agriculture on Long Island. On May 26 of that year, at the second graduation exercises, TR, Jr. was the main commencement speaker. The graduating class at the time consisted of 21 men and one, most intrepid, woman. Today, this is the 7,000-student Farmingdale State College of the State University of New York. A major building on campus is called Theodore Roosevelt Hall. [The author, who taught at this college from 1987 to 2015, greatly appreciates and warmly thanks Theodore Roosevelt, Jr., for his campus visit back in 1920!]

Ted Roosevelt had a highly successful governmental and diplomatic career. He was elected to the NYS Assembly in 1920. One year later, President Warren G. Harding appointed TR, Jr. as Assistant Secretary of the Navy—a position held by his father decades earlier and by his distant cousin, Franklin Delano Roosevelt, from 1913 to 1920. In 1924, Ted ran for the office of New York State Governor on the Republican ticket against Alfred E. Smith, the Democratic Party candidate. His distant cousin, Franklin Delano Roosevelt, criticized TR, Jr. for having a "wretched record" as Assistant Secretary of the Navy. Ted responded by saying that FDR was not a "true" Roosevelt. TR, Jr. lost that election to Alfred E. Smith. With insults thrown back and forth between the two branches of the Roosevelt family, a family feud developed. In 1929, TR, Jr. was appointed Governor of Puerto Rico and later Governor-General of The Philippines. Unfortunately, the rift between the Roosevelt family branches persisted. When FDR was inaugurated U.S. president in 1933, TR, Jr. immediately resigned from government service. In private industry, Ted Roosevelt served as Chairman of the Board of the American Express Company and as Vice President at Doubleday Books Inc. During the interim between the World Wars, TR, Jr. traveled extensively but, like his father, he always kept his home at Sagamore Hill. His classical-styled, white-colored, columned home has become a museum located several hundred feet south of TR and Edith's Victorian-styled house at the Sagamore Hill National Historic Site.

Photograph of Theodore "Ted" Roosevelt, Jr. during the 1930s.

In the prelude to the American intervention in World War II, Ted Roosevelt petitioned the U.S. Army to return to active duty. In April 1941, despite being 53 years in age, coping with poor eyesight and a weak, in fact, failing heart, TR, Jr. was back in the military uniform of a full colonel. His military attire was augmented with a cane that he needed for walking as a result of advanced arthritis. Despite his physical limitations, TR, Jr., was a superb battlefield commander. For his leadership ability, he was promoted to Brigadier General. He commanded the U.S. 4th Infantry Division. He led his men—always from the front--at the invasion of Oran, Algeria and later at the Sicily campaign. In Normandy, France, on June 6, 1944, 56-year old Brigadier General Roosevelt was the *oldest* American and the *only* general to land with the first wave of troops during the massive invasion of northern France. Unfortunately, his infantry division landed a mile and a quarter south from the designated Utah Beach landing zone. When told that essential war materiel and vehicles arrived at the proper location, over a mile away, TR, Jr. had to make a decision. Should he move his men to the materiel or have these supplies moved to where his men were now positioned. This decision had to be made with extreme urgency because TR, Jr. and his men were being raked with German machine gun fire. Without hesitation, Ted Roosevelt issued the following order: "We'll start the war from right here!" TR, Jr. exposed himself to enemy fire by serving in the dual role of commanding officer, "leading from the front of his men," and "traffic cop," directing troops and materiel to and from various locations. He performed this dual role in order to secure the landing zone, while also attempting to minimize casualties. Somehow, Ted Roosevelt escaped being hit by machine gun fire. For his bravery and leadership at Utah Beach, Roosevelt saved many lives and helped ensure the overall success of the Normandy invasion.

Theodore Roosevelt, Jr. Dies of Heart Failure 36 Days after D-Day

Thirty-six days after D-Day, Ted Roosevelt's heart unfortunately failed. Stationed with his troops in France, he passed away in the early hours of July 12, 1944. That same day, U.S. Army General Omar Bradley cut orders promoting Theodore Roosevelt, Jr. to the rank of two-star, U.S. Army Major General. (The gravestone of TR, Jr. states Brigadier General.) After the war, General Bradley was asked to name the single most heroic action he had ever seen in combat. Bradley replied: "Brigadier General Ted Roosevelt on Utah Beach." "Spit and Polish" General George Smith Patton, Jr. was at first somewhat unimpressed with TR, Jr.'s performance as a regimental commander in North Africa. However, Ted Roosevelt's bravery and command presence while leading troops in Sicily and, especially at Normandy, substantially altered Patton's opinion, who then asserted: "Theodore Roosevelt, Jr. was the bravest soldier I ever knew." TR, Jr. was buried in the Omaha Beach U.S. Military Cemetery located in *Colville Sur Mer*, France. His grave is next to his youngest brother, Quentin Roosevelt, who was killed in WWI aerial combat in July 1918.

Theodore Roosevelt, Jr.'s
grave in Normandy, France.

Theodore Roosevelt, Jr. Posthumously Awarded the "Medal of Honor"

Brigadier General Theodore Roosevelt, Jr. was posthumously awarded the U.S. Congressional Medal of Honor on September 28, 1944, by distant cousin President Franklin Delano Roosevelt. FDR said of TR., Jr.: "His father would be most proud!" The following is Theodore Roosevelt, Jr.'s U.S. Congressional Medal of Honor citation:

> For gallantry and intrepidity at the risk of his life above and beyond the call of duty on 6 June 1944, in France. After two verbal requests to accompany the leading assault elements in the Normandy invasion had been denied, Brig. Gen. Roosevelt's written request for this mission was approved and he landed with the first wave of the forces assaulting the enemy-held beaches. He repeatedly led groups from the beach, over the seawall and established them inland.

His valor, courage, and presence in the very front of the attack and his complete unconcern at being under heavy fire inspired the troops to heights of enthusiasm and self-sacrifice. Although the enemy had the beach under constant direct fire, Brig. Gen. Roosevelt from one locality to another, rallying men around him, directed and personally led them against the enemy. Under his seasoned, precise, calm, and unfaltering leadership, assault troops reduced strong points and rapidly moved inland with minimum casualties. He thus contributed substantially to the successful establishment of the beachhead in France.

The U.S. Congressional Medal of Honor
was awarded posthumously to
Brigadier General Theodore Roosevelt, Jr.
on September 24, 1944.

Photographs of Theodore Roosevelt, Jr. At left is TR, Jr. shaking hands with President Calvin Coolidge during the 1920s. Next is Brig. General Theodore Roosevelt, Jr. standing with the help of a walking cane. The third photo shows TR, Jr. wrapped in a scarf while in Normandy, France. The last photo shows Ted Roosevelt sitting on the bumper of his "Rough Rider" Jeep shortly before he died from heart failure.

The Adventurous and Troubled Life of Kermit Roosevelt

Born at Sagamore Hill on October 10, 1889, Kermit Roosevelt resembled his father in many ways: an outdoorsman, an accomplished student who completed his four-year Harvard University undergraduate degree in 2.5 years, and a prodigious writer on a vast array of subjects. Kermit accompanied his father on a safari to Africa, from 1909 to 1910, to gather specimens for the American Museum of Natural History and Smithsonian Institution. He also joined his father, in late 1913 and early 1914, in a harrowing scientific exploration of the *Río da Dúvida* (River of Doubt that was subsequently renamed *Río Roosevelt*) in the heart of the Amazon rain forest. During this trip, TR severely injured his leg while moving a canoe. TR's leg soon became infected, and the former U.S. president developed a dangerously high fever. To save his son and other expedition members, TR urged Kermit to leave him. If left alone, TR would undoubtedly have perished, either by his own hand (a revolver was ready for this purpose) or at the hands of hostile indigenous Amazonian warriors. These warriors were hostile to *intruders* out of fear and based upon past harsh treatment by those wishing to exploit Brazil's rain forests. Candice Millard (2005) writes that both expeditions that followed the TR trek were unsuccessful. The first of these expeditions was forced to turn back after being repulsed by hostile natives. The second expedition fared far worse—they were never heard from again! It is presumed the expedition members died from an accident, disease, and/or hostile Amazonian warriors. TR's expedition came close to suffering a similar fate. Injured and dehydrated with a raging fever, TR was prostrate in the middle of the Amazon. This greatly impeded the expedition at a time when food was almost depleted. TR pleaded with Kermit to leave him—then presumably TR would commit suicide. Of course, Kermit would not abandon his ailing father. Several weeks passed before TR could be moved. Even then, TR could not walk but had to be carried out of the Amazon on a stretcher.

Kermit was also a courageous soldier, who fought in World War I with the British Army in the Middle East. When the U.S.A. entered the war, he transferred to the American Expeditionary Force in France. With all of his positive attributes, Kermit was deeply troubled emotionally. His father early on detected signs of mental duress that was reminiscent of TR's younger brother Elliot, the father of Anna Eleanor Roosevelt (wife of FDR). Both Elliot and Kermit may have suffered from what was then called *black moods*. This illness would most likely be called in present day vernacular, "clinical depression." Greatly compounding their shared illness was an ever-deepening dependency on alcohol. The Theodore Roosevelt Association website mentions that TR, noting the early signs of the similar illness that affected his younger brother, Elliott, made a special effort to spend time with young Kermit. After returning home from the Great War, Kermit initially achieved success in business ventures. He also became a critically acclaimed writer with *Trailing the Great Panda* (co-authored with his older brother and fellow explorer, Theodore "Ted" Roosevelt, Jr.).

Kermit Roosevelt (1889-1943).

During the two decades between the wars, Kermit began to imbibe heavily. By the outbreak of WWII, Kermit's marriage had crumbled; and he was in the throws of alcoholism. It was hoped that a return to military life would help Kermit recover from depression and alcoholism. During World War II, Kermit once again served briefly with the British Army in the period before the United States entered the conflict. When the U.S.A. went to war in December 1941, Kermit Roosevelt was re-commissioned into the U.S. Army and was assigned to Fort Richardson, Alaska. His black moods, alcoholism, and deteriorating physical condition all worsened. Unlike 29 years earlier in the Amazon when Kermit shielded his father from a possible suicide, no one was there to stop Kermit from self-destruction. In the late evening of June 3, 1943, Kermit aimed his British Army-issued service weapon to his chin and fired. His suicide, according to the Theodore Roosevelt Association website, was withheld from his mother Edith. Instead, the story told to her and the public stated he died of a heart attack. Again quoting the website: "Not until the 1980s, well after Edith's death, was his suicide openly discussed." Kermit's brothers labeled him, ironically, the "lucky one." This is because he accompanied his wanderlust father on "splendid adventures." However, even the persuasiveness of someone as forceful as TR could not ultimately prevent Kermit from following an inexorable path to self-destruction. History reveals uncanny, tragic comparisons between TR and his sons and John Quincy Adams and his sons. In both families, the father served as U.S. president. In the subsequent generation, some sons achieved stunning success, while one or more other sons suffered through depression and alcoholism. In both families, the most troubled son committed suicide.

Ethel Carow Roosevelt Derby: Founder of Nassau County's American Red Cross

Born August 13, 1891, Ethel was the only daughter of TR's marriage to Edith. Just like her brothers, Ethel served her country with dedication. During World War I, after serving as a field nurse in France with her husband, Dr. Richard Derby, she became—and remained—heavily involved with the American Red Cross and the field of nursing. During World War II, Ethel served in the capacity as founding Chairperson of the Nassau County, New York, Chapter of the American Red Cross. After the war, she served as Chairperson of the Nassau County Nursing Service. She was—and will always be--a superb role model for others contemplating a nursing career.

Photograph of Ethel Carow Roosevelt Derby (1891-1977) in her youth and a painting of her in American Red Cross uniform.

When it came time for her to sit for a portrait, Ethel Carow Roosevelt Derby, comfortably wealthy, chose not to be painted with an evening gown or jewels. Instead, she elected to be painted in her well-worn American Red Cross uniform. Following a long-standing Roosevelt tradition, "service to country" mattered deeply to Ethel. Late in her life, the American Red Cross presented her with a "50 years of service" pin. Ethel responded with much appreciation. At the same time, she corrected the organization. Ethel accurately declared that her length of service to the American Red Cross was actually *60 years*. She was also one of the first two women to serve on the Board of Trustees of the American Museum of Natural History. Ethel is given significant credit for initiating the patriotic transfer of her family's house and surrounding grounds to the U.S. National Park Service. She lived to age 86, passing away on December 10, 1977.

Archibald Bulloch Roosevelt--"100%-Disabled" in Two World Wars

"Archie," as he was called, was born in Washington, D.C. on April 9, 1894, while his father was serving on the U.S. Civil Service Commission. Less robust than his other brothers, he became seriously—some thought gravely—ill at age 13.

Archibald Bulloch Roosevelt
(1894-1779).

Archie pulled through and set for himself a pattern of stalwart resiliency that he followed through two world wars. Captain Roosevelt was wounded three times and received numerous medals for valor in World War I. His wounds were so extensive that he was considered 100 percent disabled. Archie served again in the U.S. Army in World War II, this time as Lieutenant Colonel. He served with utmost valor and again received many decorations. As with the first war, intrepid Archie was again seriously wounded in the second war. According to the Theodore Roosevelt Association website, Archibald Roosevelt is the only U.S. soldier to have been 100 percent disabled from *two* world wars. Following World War II, he became Chairman of the Board of Roosevelt & Cross, a Wall Street investment firm. Overcoming his dual-war injuries, Archibald Bulloch Roosevelt lived to age 85, passing away on October 13, 1979.

Quentin Roosevelt — Valor in the Great War

Quentin Roosevelt, the youngest son and purportedly favorite child of Theodore Roosevelt, was born in Washington, D.C. on November 19, 1897.

Photograph of a pre-teen Quentin Roosevelt. At center is Lt. Quentin Roosevelt in his U.S. Army Air Corps uniform. At right is a monument marker honoring the young pilot. Quentin Roosevelt was buried next to his brother Ted in the Omaha Beach American Military Cemetery in *Colville Sur Mer*, France.

Twenty-year old Quentin served with valor as an aviator during World War I. Quentin had poor eyesight, as did TR and TR, Jr. Quentin:

> …Struggled with difficult flight training on Nieuport planes, already discarded by the French as a second-rate aircraft. Under brutally cold conditions, in November 1917, he caught pneumonia and was sent to Paris on a three-week leave and was derided by his older brothers, Ted, Archie and Kermit, all of whom were already on their way to the front…Quentin was determined to get to the front, to silence his brothers' criticism and prove himself to them and to his father. In June 1918, Quentin got his wish when he was made a flight commander in the 95th Aero Squadron, in action near the Aisne River… During the Second Battle of the Marne [on July 14, 1918]

his Nieuport was engaged by three Boche planes, according to one of the other pilots on his flight mission. Shot down, Quentin's plane fell behind German lines, near the village of Chamery. (www.history.com/this-day-in-history/quentin-roosevelt-killed; Retrieved 2/29/2016).

Sustaining two bullet head wounds, Quentin was dead before his plane crashed to the ground. Quentin Roosevelt was awarded the *Croix de Guerre* posthumously by the French Government. Though immensely proud of Quentin's heroism, TR was never the same after his beloved "Quinikin's" death. Edmund Morris has stated in a November 2001 speech covered by C-Span that TR died less than six months after Quentin "of a broken heart." The Westbury Plateau Flying Field in Mineola, Nassau County, New York where Quentin received his flight training was, after his death, renamed "Quentin Roosevelt Airfield." On May 20, 1927, a landmark moment in history was made at this airfield. U.S. Army Colonel Charles Augustus Lindbergh (Ret.) took off on his epic nonstop solo flight across the Atlantic Ocean from New York to Paris. Noted pilot Wiley Post also used Quentin Roosevelt Air Field for many of his record-breaking flights. Today by far the largest shopping mall in New York State (10th largest in the U.S.A.) is located at the site of this airfield. The mall is called "Roosevelt Field."

Theodore Roosevelt and Family Legacy to Long Island and the Nation

TR and his family have left a permanent, lustrous mark on Long Island and on the nation. Information has been excerpted in this essay from a number of reference sources—most notably from and with much appreciation to the Theodore Roosevelt Association. The following, however, is the assessment of the author: TR would be greatly honored by the individual achievements of his wife, Edith, and their children. TR and his descendants continue contributing and are inextricably linked to the Long Island region of New York State. The late John Gable, Director of the Theodore Roosevelt

Association, provides an appropriate Long Island description of TR: "Theodore Roosevelt was Nassau County's most famous resident."

References

Balfour, A. J. (1919) (quoted in Ignatius Valentine Chirol, *Cecil Spring Rice: In Memoriam: With Portrait.*) (http://babel.hathitrust.org/cgi/pt?id=coo1.ark:/13960/t6g16k11c;view=1up;seq=9; Retrieved 2/29/2016).

Brinkley, D. (2009). *The Wilderness Warrior: Theodore Roosevelt and the Crusade for America.* Harper.

Burrows, E. G., & Wallace, M. (1999). *Gotham: A History of New York City to 1898.* Oxford University Press.

Burton, D. H., (Ed.) (1976). *American History--British Historians.* Nelson-Hall.

Burton, D. H. (1990). *Cecil Spring Rice: A Diplomat's Life.* Associated University Presses.

Burton, D. H. (1999). *British-American Diplomacy 1895-1917: Early Years of the Special Relationship.* Krieger.

Chirol, I. V. (1919). *Cecil Spring Rice: In Memoriam: With Portrait.* (http://babel.hathitrust.org/cgi/pt?id=coo1.ark:/13960/t6g16k11c;view=1up;seq=9; Retrieved 2/29/2016).

C-SPAN. *President Clinton bestowing posthumously [U.S.] Congressional Medal of Honor to Theodore Roosevelt.* http://www.c-span.org/video/?161885-1/medal-honor-ceremony; Retrieved 2/29/2016).

Fonda Family Members (315) that have served in the U.S. military. (http://www.fonda.org/military.htm#WW20; Retrieved 2/29/2016).

Grey, E. (1925). *Twenty-Five Years: 1892-1916.* Google books.

Gwynn, S. (1929). *The letters and friendships of Sir Cecil Spring Rice.* Constable & Co.

NBC News. (2000; 2009). *Polls conducted by C-SPAN and*

reported by NBC News of 65 presidential historians and professional observers using 10 leadership characteristics. (http://www.nbcnews.com/id/29216774/ns/politics-white_house/t/list-presidential-rankings/; Retrieved 2/29/2016).

Renehan, E. J. Jr. (1998). *The Lion's Pride: Theodore Roosevelt and His Family in Peace and War.* Oxford University Press.

Roosevelt, T. (May 9, 1915). Murder on the High Seas. *Metropolitan Magazine.*

Roosevelt, T. (October 12, 1915). Speech to the Knights of Columbus "Grand Assembly" at Carnegie Hall.

Roosevelt, T. quote in (http://www.livescience.com/29383-theodore-roosevelt-national-park.html; Retrieved 2/29/2016).

Chapter 3
Commodore Joshua Barney:
U.S. Naval Hero of the American Revolution and the War of 1812/ Early American Archivist and Biographer Mary Barney

Commodore Joshua Barney (1759-1818) was an American naval officer deeply involved in both the Revolutionary War and the War of 1812. The Commodore fought against the British military during a more than four-decade naval career. During these years, Barney notated his adventures in journals, naval logs, diaries, and scrap pieces of paper. Thus, we have original source information covering Barney's life from early age through to the end of his life. Fourteen years after his 1818 death, his daughter-in-law, Mary Barney, compiled, edited and supplemented her father-in-law's disparate notes into a monograph entitled: *A Biographical Memoir of the Late Commodore Joshua Barney* (1832). The manuscript was published by the early 19th century Boston bookseller Gray and Bowen. Detailing many of the events of Barney's colorful life, the *Biographical Memoir* also includes commentaries, summaries, and reference notes authored by Mary Barney, who was a fluent writer and archivist as well as arguably one of the first American female historians. Mary Barney used uncomplicated language to describe her father-in-law's seemingly endless adventures. The Barney *Biographical Memoir* has not been reset in modern typeface. Rather, this work is available only by special order as a facsimile of the original 1832 book. Some of Mary's words and grammatical usages are archaic. The typeface is difficult to discern. In addition, there are centuries-old ink blotches obscuring some of the text. Yet, with all these flaws, the *Biographical Memoir* is a genuine original source document that has substantial value to researchers. The quotes in this essay are from the pages of the *Biographical Memoir*.

America's first two wars with Great Britain—unfortunately--resembled World Wars I and II. In each case, the first conflict did not entirely quell deep-seated resentments and divisions between the belligerent nations. Rather, the initial war was followed some decades later by a second conflict that resolved many, but not all, lingering disputes. In America's War for Independence, begun in 1775 and concluded in 1783 with the Treaty of Paris, the peace would last for less than three decades. Following the 1783 treaty, the British continued to incite Native American tribes to attack U.S. settlements. These attacks resulted in widespread bloodshed between the European settlers in America and the Native Americans. Though prohibited in the Treaty of Paris, the British maintained forts at the Old Northwest Territories that include today's states of Ohio, Indiana, Illinois, Michigan, Wisconsin, and the northeastern portion of Minnesota. The British publicly announced that their presence at the forts continued due to the American merchants' refusal to repay debts owed to Royal Crown overseas firms. Until these debts were paid, the British would remain on American territory. Retribution was also a factor. The British, especially King George III, were for many years in a state of apoplexy over losing the thirteen American colonies. However, these factors by themselves would probably not have led to an all-out conflict, the War of 1812. The most pressing disagreements between these English-speaking nations were the continued blockade of key U.S. ports by British "man-of-war" ships-of-the-line and the forced impressments of American seamen into the British Royal Navy.

<u>The American Revolutionary War</u>

At the tender age of 16, Joshua Barney joined America's Continental Navy in February 1776 as junior officer aboard the

Hornet. Under the command of Commodore Esek Hopkins, Barney took part in the March 3-4, 1776 raid for armaments and munitions at the port of New Providence on the island of Nassau in the Bahamas. The raid was necessary in order to obtain vital war materiel demanded by Continental Army General George Washington, who was leading troops besieging British-held Boston. The Second Continental Congress authorized Commodore Hopkins to retrieve this war materiel as soon as possible. Hopkins' battle plans included a two-day raid on New Providence warehouses. Hopkins issued a proclamation whereby the residents of the island were safe as long as they did not impede the Americans in gathering war materiel. Upon receiving Hopkins' proclamation, the island's bailiff gave the keys to the city to Commodore Hopkins. This raid, named after Hopkins, resulted in the Americans gaining 88 cannons, 15 mortars, and hundreds of pounds of gunpowder. After the raid, Barney, still only in his teens, was promoted to the rank of Lieutenant and appointed second-in-command of the warship, *USS Wasp*. Again he displayed valor and steady leadership under fire in the sea battle between the *Wasp* and the British brig, *Betsey*. U.S. Navy officer Barney later served in the defense of the Delaware River communities. Named after Thomas West, 3rd Baron De La Warr (1577-1618), the Delaware River extends 388 miles through the states of Delaware, Maryland, Pennsylvania, New Jersey, and New York.

In between military engagements involving battles on land and sea, Barney fell in love and married. Supplementing her father-in-law's memoirs, Mary Barney describes Honorable Gunning Bedford (father of Harriet Bedford) as well as the first meeting of her in-laws in early 1780. Mary's words in the *Memoir* are eloquent and loving:

> In the course of the winter, he [Joshua Barney] became acquainted with the family of Gunning Bedford, Esquire, a respectable Alderman of Philadelphia, and was introduced to his daughter [Harriett], a young lady of great beauty and

personal accomplishments, to whose fascinations he for the first time 'struck his colors,' and surrendered at discretion. 'None but the brave deserve the fair!' and what fair ever resisted the wooing of the brave particularly when the possessor of that character presents himself before her in all the freshness of youth and manly beauty! And few men ever possessed greater personal advantages than the subject of our allusion. (p. 82).

On March 16, 1780, Joshua Barney and Harriett Bedford were married. Barney benefited from a happy marriage and endless good luck during the War for Independence. Though he was captured and taken prisoner by the British several times, he was in every instance exchanged for a British officer held by the Americans. However, there was one important exception to these prisoner exchanges. It occurred in 1781, when Barney was captured and held at Old Mill Prison in the English city of Plymouth. In action fit for a Hollywood adventure movie, Barney risked his life by narrowly escaping from his English imprisonment. What followed were numerous "close calls" where British authorities attempted, but never succeeded, in capturing the elusive American naval officer. With stalwart determination and tireless energy, Barney made it back to America--completely exhausted but essentially unharmed.

A year later, in 1782, Barney was back in action as the commander of the Pennsylvania ship, *Hyder-Ally*. Barney's ship met in a brief sea battle with a much larger and more heavily armed British warship, *General Monk*. With immense gunnery skills, Captain Barney and his crew quickly forced the surrender of the *General Monk*. He assumed command of the warship that henceforth flew the colors of the U.S.A. Mary Barney writes about her father-in-law's stunning victory:

> The *Hyder-Ally* opened her ports and gave a well-directed broadside, which spoke her determination in a language not to be misunderstood. The enemy closed upon her immediately, and showed a disposition to board. At this critical juncture

> Captain Barney had the coolness and presence of mind to conceive, and execute on the instant, a *ruse de guerre*, to which he was unquestionably indebted for the victory that immediately followed. (p. 114).

After refitting, and with a reconstituted crew, the newly flagged American warship was assigned the task of carrying top-secret dispatches sent by the U.S. Congress to Ambassador Plenipotentiary to France, Benjamin Franklin. Barney's ship was also responsible for returning dispatches from Ambassador Franklin to Congress. Certainly, the most important of these messages was news of the Treaty of Paris, the 1783 declaration of peace between Great Britain and the United States of America.

<u>Interlude Between Wars</u>

Following the Revolutionary War, Captain Barney foundered badly like one of his battle-ravaged warships. Mary Barney laments: "Captain Barney was not, like most of his brother-officers in both branches of the service, returning to a mode of life with which he had been previously familiar, but was now to begin a course of action totally different from all the habits of his youth and manhood" (p. 114). Serving continuously in the navy from age 16, and for decades that followed, Barney knew of no other life than that of a naval warrior. What could top this for excitement and adventure? The answer was obvious--very little. He undertook several commerce ventures—all of which resulted in what Mary Barney characterized as "heavy losses." She adds that her father-in-law was the proverbial "fish out of water." Bored in the confines of Baltimore, in 1787, Barney set out on an overland trip that crossed the Allegheny Mountains to Fort Pitt (today's Pittsburgh). He then traveled to Wheeling in Virginia (now West Virginia). Finally, he reached the property he purchased in Kentucky. Although he enjoyed the adventure of living in the wilderness, he also felt unfulfilled. He then returned home to Baltimore.

Soon, however, his interest was piqued by national politics. On

September 17, 1787, delegates from the 13 original states began meeting in Philadelphia to revise the hastily written "Articles of Confederation." The delegates soon came to the conclusion that any revision of the "Articles of Confederation" would be wholly ineffectual in establishing a sufficiently empowered central government. Thus, the convention delegates in the "City of Brotherly Love" embarked on a new course of action: the drafting of a comprehensive document that became the U.S. Constitution. The document established the three equal branches of the federal government. To satisfy those fearful of a too-strong central government, ten amendments were added called the "Bill of Rights." Barney attended the Constitutional Convention in Philadelphia. Following the approval of the document by the convention delegates, the next task was to convince each state to ratify the document. To this end, Barney strongly advocated for the ratification of the U.S. Constitution in his home state of Maryland. To accomplish this, Barney made numerous public appearances and speeches, especially in Baltimore, advocating adoption of the document. At one of these events, an unknown assailant struck him with some sort of sharpened weapon. This injury proved to be serious and ended his public appearances. However, Barney's efforts on behalf of the document proved to be successful. On April 28, 1788 the State of Maryland formally adopted the U.S. Constitution.

Following the Constitutional Convention, Barney visited retired General Washington during the short lull of time before the "Master of Mount Vernon" was asked to be U.S. president. Mary Barney writes: "The Commodore made sail out of Baltimore harbor, and coasted along the right bank of the Chesapeake, until he came to the Potomac. His ship then ascended that river to the modest and embowered retreat of the great *Pater Patriae*. Mount Vernon was the *ultima Thule* of his expedition" (p. 158). Captain Barney was well known to George Washington, who respected and viewed the young sea warrior as a surrogate son. Barney also became a favorite of Martha Washington. When the future first, First Lady visited Baltimore, she requested that Captain Barney accompany her to New-York City (then spelled with a hyphen). By the late 1780s, Barney had earned a reputation as a national hero for his bravery in numerous sea battles. With this acclaim, he ascended into the upper echelons of America's social classes. One of the social connections Barney made was with Liverpool-born American merchant Robert Morris. Known as the "Financier of the Revolution," Morris yielded tremendous influence in Pennsylvania and was instrumental in having Barney receive appointment offers to two important positions, including Captain of a U.S. Revenue Cutter and Clerk of the District Court of Maryland. Barney viewed himself as a sea warrior and not as a tax enforcer. Thus, he declined the former position. He accepted the second offer but was bored and quit the position after a short time.

Then the sea captain, with a partner, purchased a warehouse that stored cargo that he could ship in his own vessel. Mary Barney writes that in the 1790s her father sailed back and forth from Baltimore to the Caribbean. Included among his ports of call were Cape François, Haiti; Cartagena, Colombia; and Havana, Cuba. He was happy to command a ship at sea. No doubt, he also enjoyed, perhaps for the first time in his life, earning a sizable income. However, on one trip to Haiti, he was nearly killed when revolutionaries fighting French government rulers attacked his cargo ship. Before fleeing war-ravaged Haiti, Barney heroically allowed many women and children to board his ship for safety. However, the terror of this voyage did not end there. En route back to Baltimore, Barney and his crew became prisoners of privateers sanctioned by the British government. As he did previously, Barney somehow escaped from his captors. He then returned to his embargoed ship and sailed back to Baltimore. Undeterred, Barney made further journeys to war torn Haiti—this time to Cape François. Unlike in his previous voyages, his ship was now armed with cannons. Barney also obtained from the French government a "Letter of Marque." This document gave Barney formal authority to seize vessels from nations at war with France, most especially those of Great Britain. Barney at this point in time was militarily aligned with the French government as a legally sanctioned "privateer." Unfortunately, Barney was subsequently once again captured by the British and charged with piracy. He was put on trial in the British colony of Jamaica. Through lack of evidence that he was a pirate, and with an immense outpouring of support from the American government, Barney was acquitted.

After the bloody despot Maximilien Robespierre was driven from power and executed on July 28, 1795, Barney accepted a commission as Commodore of the French Navy. During his tenure as head of the French fleet, Barney escaped battle wounds though he was injured, in 1796, when rough seas threw him under one of his ship's cannons. His injury was a severe break in his thighbone that never entirely healed. Beginning in 1797, while serving as French Commodore, Barney owned his own fleet of cargo ships that delivered goods to port cities in France. His trading enterprise proved initially lucrative. However, before long, he became embroiled in a long-running financial dispute with French businessmen and, subsequently, the French government. Barney sued for the payment of $32,000 for wheat and coffee cargoes delivered at several French cities. Though Barney was wise and diplomatic enough to not antagonize the new French ruler, Napoleon Bonaparte, the American sailor/businessman became increasingly hostile dealing with corrupt French government ministers. These ministers were overtly dishonest in demanding bribes from Barney. The American refused to submit bribe money in order for his case to be handled in the French legal system. After repeated offers to resign his commission, the French government finally accepted his resignation in 1802. Barney was extremely happy to end his nearly decade long association with the French government and navy. However, he was still entangled in lawsuits and counter claims. His legal battles spread to America. French government officials were in the process of legally seizing his home in Baltimore in lieu of payment. These legal tussles continued until the end of 1804, when Barney was absolved from his debts in France. He also finally received the full payment of the monies he was owed. This was a payment of 300,000 francs (equivalent to $56,000).

In 1805, President Thomas Jefferson offered Barney the position of Superintendent of the recently established naval yards located in Washington City. He was also appointed to the rank of Commodore. In 1806, a group of Maryland's esteemed citizens urged Barney to run for a congressional seat representing the city and county of Baltimore. Although he won a majority of votes in the city of Baltimore, his opponent for the congressional seat won the majority of votes in the county of Baltimore. With this split vote, the Federal government became involved by forming a committee to resolve the dispute. The congressional committee ultimately decided that Barney's political opponent, William McCreery, was the winner.

Mrs. Harriet Barney, long afflicted with rheumatism, was at a stage where she was unable to walk unassisted. Without asking for help, Harriet attempted to walk a short distance herself. Disoriented, she fell down and broke several bones in her legs. Although she somewhat recovered from her injuries, her health deteriorated in 1808. She succumbed to her illnesses in July of that year at the age of fifty-four.

The family of Joshua Barney was accustomed to him being away due to long sea voyages, not to mention his nearly decade long tenure as Privateer for, and then Commodore of, the French Navy. Two years after his first wife died, Barney remarried. As in 1806, he was again urged to run for the congressional seat representing Baltimore in 1810. As occurred four years earlier, he attained the majority of votes in the city of Baltimore, but not in the wider geographical district of the county of Baltimore. The election went to his political opponent, Alexander McKim. After these two attempts to become elected to political office, Barney swore that he would never again delve into politics. He kept that oath during the remaining eight years of his life.

The War of 1812

The recurring Napoleonic wars persisted during the Jefferson and Madison Administrations. During this time, the British Navy had a virtually endless demand for seamen in their huge navy. To this end, British warships were intercepting American cargo vessels at sea and impressing, that is kidnapping, American seamen on the dubious rationale that these sailors were Royal Navy deserters. In fact, very few British sailors had deserted to American ships. The British also were claiming, erroneously, that the Americans were allying with the French. After repeated complaints to the British to stop these practices, the British refused. On June 18, 1812, the U.S. Congress declared war on Great Britain. Adding to the tensions between the countries were actions of the so-called American "War Hawks," led by Speaker of the U.S. House of Representatives Henry Clay (1777-1852). One of the principal aims of the "War Hawks" was the conquest of Canada. The "War Hawks" espoused a woefully irrational belief that Canadians would leave British sovereignty and join the United States. Vince Vaise, Fort McHenry National Monument and Historic Shrine Park (Maryland) Ranger and Interpreter, has remarked that the only tangible consequence of the Canadian invasions was a large group of Americans residing in Canadian prisons. Adding to the confusion and discord during the War of 1812 was the fact that the New England states, constituting a major region of the U.S.A., deliberately and overtly refrained from supporting the rest of the country in this conflict dubbed, "Mr. Madison's War." Though there were some major sea victories for the Americans, the overwhelming number of land battles resulted in defeats and catastrophic loss of life.

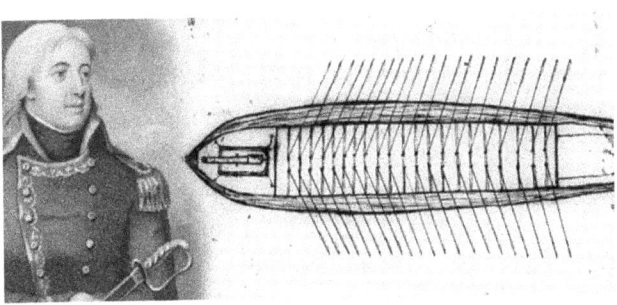

Commodore Joshua Barney and an ink drawing of his design for the Chesapeake gunboats that comprised his *Flotilla*.

Beginning on July 12, 1812, Joshua Barney commanded the privateer vessel, *Rossie*. During the summer of 1813, Barney received a letter from William Jones, U.S. Secretary of the Navy, offering him a commission of U.S. Navy Commodore and the command of the *Flotilla*. As the name implies, the *Flotilla* would consist of a fleet of small gunboats and barges that would be designed, built, and armed according to Barney's instructions. By April 1814, Barney had under his command nine hundred sailors and twenty-six small vessels. Over the coming months, these vessels with their shallow drafts would prove to be indispensable in defending the Chesapeake Bay and Patuxent River. One of his officers was his son, Major William B. Barney. On June 1, 1814, Barney's *Flotilla* attacked a fleet of British ships at the mouth of the Patuxent River. Joining in the sea battle was a mammoth British ship-of-the-line, the huge 74-cannon *Dragon*. During the first week of June 1814, Barney would stage "hit and run" attacks on the British ships. However, on June 8 and the days to follow, Barney's *Flotilla* sustained major damage in a battle that lasted two days. One of Barney's barges took a direct hit from a British rocket, resulting in the vessel being set alit and much of the crew injured with several deaths. However, the large British ships could not sail into inlets, which had very shallow depths.

Frustrated and seeking retribution, the British burnt nearly all the neighboring farms and mills in the shoreline areas in what has been called the Battle of St. Leonard's Creek (today's St. Leonard Creek, Maryland spelled without an "s"). Secretary of the Navy Jones ordered a contingent of 106 U.S. Marines to directly aid Commodore Barney. After the first attack, U.S. Secretary of War John Armstrong ordered six hundred army soldiers and several pieces of heavy cannon to be transferred to areas surrounding St. Leonard's Creek. The British Royal Army and Navy again attacked St. Leonard's Creek, this time on June 26. According to the *Memoir*: "The conduct of the U.S. Army 38th regiment, under Colonel Carberry, was unfortunately but little more worthy of praise than that of the militia [who fled the battle scene]: though several of its officers were well disposed to meet the enemy upon any terms, the men had neither discipline nor subordination, and receiving no check from their commanding officer gave themselves up to disgraceful inaction, so that the presence of this regiment added nothing to the effective force of the Commodore" (p. 259). This was an entirely different situation in relation to the U.S. Marines. Under the heroic leadership of U.S. Marine Captain Samuel Miller, Barney had brave, reliable fighters. The British withdrew temporarily until August 16, at which point some British warships had again entered the Patuxent River.

Battle of Bladensburg

On August 18, 1814, the British infantry invaded the port village of Benedict on the southern shore of Maryland. The aim of the British was now clear. They intended to march 25 miles north and attack Washington City. Secretary of War Armstrong was grossly negligent in inadequately preparing for the defense of the capital city. On the evening of August 23, President Madison camped near the scene of the battle. In command of the American forces was Brigadier General William Winder. In his *Memoir*, Barney excoriates Winder: "On the morning of the 24th the commanding U.S. general—if, indeed, he could be properly so called had an interview with the Commodore" (p. 264). Winder was bewildered as to what to do: attack, defend, or retreat? Winder dithered until it was too late. The British Army, led by General Robert Ross, quickly overwhelmed the American militia defenders at Benedict. The Americans retreated to Bladensburg, Maryland, where they would make a "last stand" blocking the British from overrunning the capital city. Joining in the fight with the U.S. Army and Maryland State Militiamen were Commodore Barney and his 360 U.S. Navy sailors—now battling on land as infantrymen. U.S. Marines Corps Captain Miller led a 106-man rifle company that fought alongside Commodore Barney's sailors. The British invaders greatly outnumbered the American forces. A significant number of the U.S. Army and militia officers were killed in the battle. At that point, many U.S. soldiers and militiamen panicked and fled the battlefield. Thus, the Battle of Bladensburg has become known in history, derisively, as the "Bladensburg Races."

Now the Commodore, his 360 sailors, and a 106-man U.S. Marine rifle company were all that stood in the way of thousands of British invaders from capturing the capital city. For hours, Barney's sailors and U.S. Marines bravely cannonaded and fought hand-to-hand with the British. Though these brave Americans enacted substantial casualties upon the Royal armed forces, the U.S. servicemen were greatly outnumbered. Nearly all of these sailors and Marines were either killed or wounded. Commodore Barney was shot in the thigh and fell near a cannon. After defeating the Americans, Admiral Sir George Cockburn and General Robert Ross soon came upon a seriously wounded, incapacitated Barney. Though a long time enemy, Barney was highly regarded as a brave, unflappable foe by the British. When General Ross and Admiral Cockburn approached the wounded, prostrate Barney, the British General remarked: "I am really very glad to see you, Commodore!" to which the American Commodore replied: "I am sorry I cannot return you the compliment, General!" General Ross smiled, and turning to Admiral Cockburn, remarked, "I told you it was the *Flotilla* men!" (p. 267). In respect to Barney, the British commanders immediately paroled Barney to their surgeons so that the bullet in his thigh could be extricated. Unfortunately, the bullet fused with his thighbone and could not be removed. With Barney incapacitated and his sailors and U.S. Marines overwhelmed, the last defense for protecting Washington City was eliminated.

After Burning the American Capital, the British Suffer Stinging Defeats

The British invaders entered and torched much of the capital city, including the Executive Mansion. After these despicable actions, the British left the same way they entered Maryland, at the small port village of Benedict. The British now presumed that Baltimore, like the capital city, was going to be easily conquered.

Within three weeks, however, the British suffered several stinging defeats. On September 11, 1814, U.S. Navy Master Commandant Thomas Macdonough led an American task force of ships that defeated the British Royal Navy, who invaded Lake Chaplain at the Battle of Plattsburgh in northern New York State.

The next day, in an entirely separate military engagement, the British invaded North Point, Maryland. The invaders were attempting to torch Baltimore, as they had done in Washington City. Unlike the defenses of Washington City, which were inadequate and disorganized, Baltimore was heavily defended. At the command of the forces were two highly effective military leaders. Maryland State Militia Brigadier General John S. Stricker was in charge. His militiamen fought bravely--nearly to the last man--in slowing down the British at the Battle of North Point. At this battle, British General Robert Ross, who offered a "warm welcome" to the wounded Commodore Barney at Bladensburg, was killed. Slowed but not stopped, the British moved literally to the entrance of Baltimore. Here, the Americans prepared robust breastworks fortified with many cannon emplacements. In overall command of the American defenders of Baltimore was a highly experienced soldier, Maryland State Militia Major General Samuel Smith. His land defenses guarding Baltimore proved to be insurmountable. The British suffered catastrophic losses and were forced to withdraw from Baltimore.

Blocking Baltimore Harbor were a large number of American merchant ships deliberately sunk to form a physical barrier. Guarding the harbor was Fort McHenry. Major General Samuel Smith assigned Major George Armistead to defend the fort. In 1813, Brigadier General Stricker and Commodore Barney placed an order for a small storm flag and a huge garrison flag with an expert seamstress, Mary Young Pickersgill of Baltimore. The flags had been earlier requested by Major Armistead to serve two different functions. The smaller storm flag was made with heavier weight material so that it could be flown during inclement weather.

However, it was the much larger garrison flag that would become the symbol of American courage and tenacity. The British Royal Navy bombarded Fort McHenry for 25 consecutive hours from September 13 to September 14, 1814. When the bombardment ended, the defenders of the fort raised the gigantic U.S.A. garrison flag. This symbol of American defiance was, of course, the iconic Star-Spangled Banner. Within hours of seeing the huge U.S.A. flag, the British determined that Fort McHenry, and thus Baltimore, could not be conquered either by land or by sea. One by one, the British ships left the Chesapeake Bay never to return. The War of 1812 officially ended with the December 24, 1814 signing of the Treaty of Ghent. However, word of the peace treaty did not reach North America until after the Battle of New Orleans in January 1815. At this pivotal battle at the mouth of the Mississippi River, General Andrew Jackson led an army of Americans of mixed races, religions, and ethnic backgrounds in fighting a large-scale British invasion army. Jackson and his American defenders nearly annihilated the British Royal Army. General Sir Edward Packenham, overall commander of the British forces, was killed on the first day of the weeklong battle that raged from January 8 through January 15, 1815. Almost all of the remaining high-ranking British officers were also killed in the battle that claimed the lives of an estimated 2,000 British grenadiers.

Commodore Barney After the War of 1812

Following the War of 1812, Barney was honored for his bravery at many ceremonies in various cities, especially in his hometown of Baltimore. Decades before the war, Barney purchased land in Kentucky. Upon his retirement, he finally planned to relocate there permanently. However, his lingering thigh wound was immensely painful; and it often immobilized him. After repeated unsuccessful attempts to extract the bullet from Barney, surgeons recommended that he "live with the bullet" imbedded in his thigh. Withstanding much pain, Barney finally felt well enough to embark upon his journey to Kentucky. While en route, Barney suffered violent spasms in his injured leg, most likely from pulmonary embolisms. The last of these seizures ended his life on December 10, 1818. He died in Pittsburgh and was buried in nearby Allegheny Cemetery. Mary Barney concludes the *Memoir* of her father-in-law as follows:

> His inferiors and dependents, of every class, revered and loved him with a sincerity of attachment that nothing but death could have dissolved. Such was the character of Joshua Barney. If, in this delineation, we have avoided bringing into view any of the failings, from which, as a human being, he could not have been exempt, it is not because we have desired to represent him as a 'faultless monster'—but because those, whom they most nearly concerned, and who alone could have been injured by them, were prompt to forgive and forget them, in the contemplation of his nobler qualities. (p. 301)

Barney, M. (Editor and Commentator, 1832). *A Biographical Memoir of the Late Commodore Joshua Barney*. Boston: Gray and Bowen.

Chapter 4
Dolley Payne Madison:
"First Lady as the Mother of the Nation"

Dolley Payne Todd (1768-1849)
about the time she wed James Madison.

Dolley, spelled with an "e," lived from May 20, 1768 until July 12, 1849. During her event-filled lifetime, she experienced firsthand the American Revolution, the difficult birth and early years of the new nation, devastating Yellow Fever epidemics, and the onset of the national two-party political system. In August 1814, she came close to being captured as a result of her heroic efforts to save government documents and the cherished Gilbert Stuart portrait of George Washington. Dolley changed the course of American history through charismatic power. She had the rare ability to influence individuals through charm, intuition, and wit. Her iconic image of strolling through throngs of invited guests—both political friends and foes of her husband's administration--at her salons, affectionately known as "Squeezes," offered a dynamic vision. This was of an engaging woman, clad with fashionable high-waisted gowns and multicolored turbans accented by bird-of-paradise plumes. Beyond the image, she considered the role of "First Lady" to be "Mother of the Nation" (http://www.biography.com/people/dolley-madison-9394952; Retrieved 2/29/2016). Importantly, she was the caring wife and life partner to the nation's fourth president, James Madison (1751-1836).

Yet, these observations do not completely describe her persona because missing is "Dolley, the survivor." She was someone who had suffered numerous tragedies in her life. Her steadfast resolve and her perseverance would overcome the heartache of losing nearly her entire family due to alcoholism, epidemics, sea calamities, and even murder. Dolley's only surviving son, John Payne Todd, was an alcoholic, gambler, and spendthrift. He squandered what little wealth she possessed during her later years. These setbacks, which could have been debilitating, instead strengthened her resolve throughout her 81-year life. Dolley excelled as America's First Lady because she essentially *created* that role, many elements of which exist to the present day. At the same time, she took care of her frequently ill, though always brilliant "Great Little Madison." After his death in 1836, she lived her remaining years struggling with meager finances. Though coping with little money, Dolley was encouraged by the universal respect and appreciation she earned from her fellow Americans. Dolley once overheard Speaker of the House Henry Clay quip: "Everybody loves Mrs. Madison." Dolley, reacting quickly, answered: "This is because Mrs. Madison loves everybody!"

Dolley's beauty in her youth remained with her throughout her entire life. Shielded from the sun in her early years by Quaker bonnets, she possessed perfect alabaster skin and Irish blue eyes framed by luscious, raven-black colored curly hair. Dolley's mother, Mary Coles, was mainly of Irish heritage with some Scottish and Welsh blood in the mix. Her father, John Payne, was of English stock. Her parents were married in Hanover County of the Virginia Colony in 1761. Three years later, they applied for membership in the Quaker community. Although Mary was a birthright Quaker, that is, born to Quaker parents, John's parents were of the Episcopalian faith. Thus, to be accepted as a Quaker, John was required to undergo a yearlong conversion process. During this time, Quaker elders fully investigated the "fitness" of John to be accepted as a Quaker Friend. The Quakers were fervently devoted to hard work, honesty, and simplicity in dress and lifestyle. They also believed in abstinence from alcohol and were strongly against slavery. The Quakers believed in a strict adherence to the social mores and edicts of the elders of their religious sect. Addressing each other as "Friend," the Quakers also frequently spoke using the archaic English "thee" and "thou." The Quakers had large communities in the Virginia, North Carolina, and Pennsylvania colonies. English Quaker leader William Penn (1644-1718) founded his colony as an American sanctuary, which protected "freedom of conscience" in terms of religious beliefs.

Payne Family Settles in Pennsylvania

In 1765, the Payne family members were admitted into the Quaker Cedar Creek Monthly Meeting located in the northeastern part of the Virginia Colony. By the end of that year, the couple along with their three-year old son, Walter, moved south to the New Garden Quaker settlement in the Piedmont area of the North Carolina Colony. The Payne family also brought with them slaves to tend their farm. Slavery, an anathema to fundamental Quaker beliefs, posed a major dilemma for the Payne family. Do they obey Quaker edicts or risk financial ruin? This question would haunt

Dolley's father until the end of his life. While in North Carolina, Dolley's second oldest brother, William Temple Payne, was born on June 17, 1766. Dolley was born two years later. Although her father farmed while in Virginia, he chose to be classified within the North Carolina Quaker community as a "merchant." Unsuccessful, he faced mounting debts and was forced to bring his family back to Virginia.

By the spring of 1769, the Paynes returned to the Old Dominion reunited with their extended family and the Cedar Creek Quakers. They lived there for fourteen years, an interval that included the tumultuous time of the American Revolution. As a Quaker, John Payne was forbidden to take up arms. While not a combatant, the war nevertheless directly affected him and his family. The Quakers were acknowledged neutrals in the conflict. However, this did not stop many non-Quakers from viewing the religious sect as being pro-Loyalist. Adding to difficulties with his southern neighbors was John Payne's strong views against the institution of slavery. He coupled his views with firm action against slavery. In 1778, John Payne began freeing his slaves. By 1783, all of his slaves were free; and the family moved to Philadelphia--a city within the colony founded by Quaker leader William Penn.

Dolley Marries and Faces Tragic Losses

As the temporary capital of the new nation during the 1790s, Philadelphia was teeming with political action and with politicians. As a buxom, strikingly pretty young lady in this cosmopolitan city, Dolley soon had many admirers. However, her father narrowed the field of suitors. In 1788, John Payne began pressing Dolley to marry fellow Quaker, John Todd, Jr. Her future husband, a practicing attorney, was also to become a financial partner with Dolley's father. John Payne struggled to eke out a living manufacturing and selling laundry starch. Despite the cash infusion made by John Todd to the business, the enterprise went bankrupt in 1789. Unable to pay his creditors, John Payne was publicly shamed by being disowned by the Quaker community. John Todd's investment in the Payne family business was lost, but his engagement with Dolley continued. They were married on January 7, 1790. A little over two years later, the couple had their first child, John Payne Todd, who was born on leap year day in 1792. On October 24 of that year, Dolley's father, already deeply disconsolate, died. Walter Payne, Dolley's oldest brother, perished while at sea. He was onboard a ship that sank sometime in 1784 or 1785. In July 1793, a son to John and Dolley Todd named William Temple Todd was born. In October of that year, Philadelphia became the epicenter of a Yellow Fever epidemic. Both of Dolley's in-laws died of the plague. Three-month old William Temple Todd died from Yellow Fever on October 14, 1793. Ten days later--and exactly one year after her father died—her husband John Todd died of the fever. Family tragedies mounted. Within the next 15 months, two of Dolley's brothers died--William Temple Payne, who was lost at sea, and Isaac Payne, who was shot to death.

Dolley and her mother faced anxious creditors, who were still owed money from the failed business venture of John Payne and John Todd, Jr. To help pay these debts, Dolley's mother, Mary Coles Payne, turned the ground floor of the Payne home into a boarding house beginning in 1791. One of the boarders was Revolutionary War hero, Colonel Aaron Burr, who was then serving as Senator from New York State. Colonel Burr, a practicing attorney, offered his help as legal advisor to Dolley Payne Todd regarding her child, John Payne Todd. The Todd family wanted to take away Payne Todd due to Dolley's meager financial circumstances. Burr, who later became Vice President, and in 1804 shot Alexander Hamilton in a duel, was appointed legal guardian of Payne Todd on May 13, 1794. As had Dolley, Burr suffered the loss of loved ones. His wife, Theodosia Bartow Prevost Burr died of stomach cancer in 1794. Burr's daughter, Theodosia Burr Alston, aged 29, was lost at sea sometime in 1813. Surprisingly, there is no indication that Burr and Dolley—both widowed, single parents living in close proximity--ever formed a romantic relationship. Colonel Burr did, however, play a pivotal role in Dolley's life by introducing his congressional colleague to her.

Portrait of Aaron Burr (1756-1836).

Dolley Madison! Alass!

Dolley was still grieving over family losses in May 1794 when Colonel Burr introduced to her his colleague, James Madison, the intellectual force behind the U.S. Constitution and the Bill of Rights. The Quaker widow and congressman from Virginia were immediately smitten with each other. At first examination, the couple seemed to be of polar-opposite personalities. Dolley was exuberant, gregarious, and vivacious. On the other hand, James was quiet, reflective, and overtly reticent. Dolley dressed with high style and much color; James wore only conservative black suits. Even without her trademark, feather-plumed turbans, Dolley stood several inches taller than the diminutive, sickly-looking bookworm. As Dolley pondered her future and that of her nearly two-year-old son, she sought the marital advice of Martha Washington. That summer Martha told Dolley that Madison would make a "good husband" and it was "all the better for he being much older." James and Dolley were married on Monday, September 15, 1794, at Harewood House, the Virginia home of George Washington's nephew, George Steptoe Washington (who was wed to Dolley's younger sister, Lucy). No doubt, James Madison chose this particular day because his parents were also married on September 15—forty-five years earlier. Dolley wrote a letter to her friend, Eliza Collins Lee, the day of her wedding. The future First Lady signed the letter as follows: "Dolley Payne Todd—Evening—Dolley Madison! Alass! Over the years, there have been many interpretations of what she meant by "Alass!" Here are some more. "Alass" may have meant that she grew impatient waiting for her marriage to take place. More likely, however, it meant she *now* was married to her soul mate—the "Great Little Madison!"

Portrait of James Madison
(1751-1836).

The Quaker community was discontent with this marital union. Since Dolley married a non-Quaker, the Quaker community "disowned" her. In 1797, James Madison's congressional term came to an end and the couple "retired" to their peaceful, sprawling Virginia plantation called "Montpelier." (Though James Madison spelled his estate, "Montpellier," subsequent owners have used one "l".) Madison's mentor and close friend, Thomas Jefferson, would interrupt the Madison family's tranquil life at Montpelier in 1801. The presidential election of November 1800 was the most hotly disputed and contested in American history. The problem stemmed from the tally of the Democratic-Republican Party. Both Jefferson and Burr were tied in the tally with each having 73 votes. After an additional four months of tied votes by electors and by members of congress, the deadlock was broken on February 17, 1801. This occurred when several Federalists, led by Representative James A.

Bayard of Delaware, cast "blank" votes. Formerly, Bayard and some Federalists voted for Burr. With the abstention of these Federalists, Burr's vote tally was reduced thereby giving Jefferson a winning majority. The iconic author of the Declaration of Independence was now President of the United States, and Burr was now Vice President. Soon after being inaugurated, Jefferson requested James Madison to serve as his Secretary of State. Madison was sworn into this position on May 2, 1801. Dolley, as well as being the wife of the Secretary of State, would soon have additional responsibilities.

Jefferson began to have formal dinners and gatherings, where invited guests attended in the company of their wives. Following protocol, women could not attend these gatherings unless a hostess was present. As Jefferson was a widower, the role of hostess fell to his adult daughter, Polly. Although Martha "Polly" Jefferson Randolph at times did fill in as hostess, it was Dolley Madison, who, on May 27, was formally asked, via presidential request, to serve in this vital role. The presidential "call-to-duty" letter to Dolley came just 25 days after her husband was sworn in as Secretary of State. While the position of hostess was unofficial, the importance entailed in this role was substantial. Dolley, with a combination of glowing beauty, ebullient personality, gentle humor, and overall charm, made a superb hostess. The former Quaker had a keen ability to remember names, events, and personal details about her guests. She also had an uncanny way with people that mitigated potentially uncomfortable, embarrassing situations--all in an entertaining and respectful way. By displaying genuine goodwill toward her guests, she had a quelling effect on individuals who may have been hostile—for one reason or another—toward the Jefferson Administration. However, her duties as unofficial U.S. Hostess were put on hold in 1805. This is when her knee became inflamed. She feared amputation. After a convalescence of several weeks in Philadelphia, the ulcer on her knee heeled; and she was able to resume her role as hostess. Though her knee ailment improved, she began to have problems with her eyes. Her self-indulgent, wayward son, Payne Todd, also troubled her. Her son's miscreant behavior would plague her for the rest of her life. Between 1806 and 1808, Dolley faced the loss of two nieces, her mother, Mary Coles Payne, and her 26-year old sister, Mary Coles Payne Jackson. While grieving internally the deaths of her family members, Dolley continued to maintain her ever-pleasant outward persona toward guests throughout this period.

James Madison was the Democratic-Republican Party presidential candidate in 1808. He won the election that year by a wide margin. After serving eight years as unofficial hostess during the Jefferson presidency, Dolley would serve as First Lady when her husband was president from 1809 until 1817. She poured much effort into bringing people together whether they were allies or political foes of her husband. During these eight years, Dolley essentially created the standard of performance for First Ladies as the "Mother of Her Nation." One example of this standard is how well or poorly the First Lady is received by the general public. Dolley, in this respect, arguably stands above all others, with perhaps Eleanor Roosevelt being an exception. Dolley's successor, Elizabeth Kortright Monroe did not—albeit unjustly--fare well in this respect. What about Dolley's predecessors Martha Washington and Abigail Adams? There is absolutely no doubt that they were accomplished, distinctive individuals in many ways. [One of the essays to follow in this book points out in detail the important role of Martha Washington in the Revolutionary War!] However, neither of Dolley's predecessors, and only a very few of her successors, has had as great an influence on national and international politics as Dolley. Each week she charmed and swayed key congressional decision makers and foreign diplomats at her innovative Executive Mansion gatherings. She also served a new culinary invention called "ice cream" at these events. Her soirees were so successful that they topped the list of Washington City social events. With throngs of attendees crammed into the home of the president, Dolley's gatherings earned the sobriquet: "Squeezes." Dolley's abilities to charm and influence decision makers were clearly noticed. The newspapers worldwide began referring to her as

"Lady Presidentress" or simply "The Presidentress."

America Fights Again for Its Independence

James Madison's presidential predecessors attempted to steer away from war with Great Britain and France--the two great super powers during the seventeenth and eighteenth centuries. Measures such as the 1794 Jay Treaty, during the Washington Administration, and the Embargo Act of December 1807, during the Jefferson Administration, were instituted to avoid conflict with these highly militarized countries. However, disputes, especially with Great Britain, persisted. The British Royal Army continued to occupy forts that were no longer permitted in the 1783 Treaty of Paris that ended the Revolutionary War. The Royal Navy, recurrently short the required number of sailors for fighting the Napoleonic Wars at sea, was "impressing" American seamen by the thousands. The British were also stirring up trouble with Native American tribes in many regions along and within U.S. borders. For these reasons, Congress passed a declaration of war on Great Britain on June 1, 1812. The president signed this document into law seventeen days later.

Declaring a war, and effectively fighting a war, against the combined might of the British Royal Army and Navy were two distinct events for the Americans. For most of the first years of the War of 1812, the Americans were defeated on land, although victorious at sea. On July 17, 1812, the British Army captured Fort Mackinac in the Michigan Territory. Thirty days later, Brigadier William Hull surrendered Fort Detroit to the intimidating British Redcoats without any resistance. However, the U.S. Navy achieved a stunning string of victories. On August 19, the *USS Constitution* defeated the British ship, *HMS Guerriere*. Just over two months later, on October 25, the *HMS Macedonia* was captured by the *USS United States*. The *USS Constitution* was victorious again, this time on December 29, in defeating the *HMS Java*. However, the Americans overreached the next year. On April 27, 1813, a poorly led and disorganized invasion of the Canadian city of York resulted in an unmitigated disaster. In addition to large numbers of casualties, including civilians, there was widespread looting by Americans in this provincial capital of Canada. The York raid also engendered in the British a deep-seated need for exacting retribution—which did occur.

Less than 16 months later, the British got their revenge. In August 1814, the Royal Navy sailed up the Chesapeake Bay and landed troops on the shores of Maryland. The British soundly defeated the Americans who were fleeing the scene in a virtual rout [except for Commodore Barney, his sailors, and U.S. Marines—see previous essay] referred to as the Battle of Bladensburg. On August 24, 1814, finally overrunning Barney's men, the British infantry marched, unimpeded, to the center of the American capital city. At three o'clock that day, Dolley received an urgent message warning her to flee the Executive Mansion or face becoming captured as a prisoner of war. With a message as threatening as this, most individuals would have indeed escaped to safety, though not this First Lady! With courage and patriotism, Dolley refused to run for safety. Although fearing for her life, she felt an innate responsibility towards her nation. Dolley was determined to save as many important papers and artifacts housed at the Executive Mansion as possible, regardless of the danger. First among these valuables was the life-sized portrait of George Washington painted by Gilbert Stuart in 1796. As the painting, also known as the "Landsdowne Portrait," was huge and heavy, its wooden frame was screwed directly into the wall. There was not enough time to unscrew the frame. Instead, the First Lady ordered the frame to be broken apart with an axe thereby freeing the canvas. The painting could then be more easily transported. Dolley sensed that the British would use the iconic image of George Washington for propaganda purposes. She also spared from confiscation piles of official cabinet papers detailing vital information that could be used by the British against U.S interests. Besides the Stuart portrait and official documents, she retrieved Executive Mansion silverware and red velvet drapes that were designed by Benjamin Henry Latrobe. With her priorities in saving national treasures, rather than caring for herself, Dolley barely escaped being captured. Her actions demonstrated selflessness and patriotism.

By the end of this horrific day, many of the official buildings of the capital city were torched and now stood as burned ruins. Dolley genuinely feared for the life of her beloved Madison. Fortunately, she was able to briefly see the hard-pressed President later that night. Knowing each other was safe provided some relief from the appalling calamity they had just experienced. Four days after the event, the beleaguered first couple was exhausted but at last finally united. However, good news would be announced two weeks later. U.S. ground and naval forces defeated the British at the Battle of Plattsburgh in northern New York State. As a consequence, the vitally strategic Lake Champlain would remain under U.S. control. The British were also stymied in their conquest of Baltimore. The stalwart defenders at Fort McHenry, a sizable star-shaped structure that guards Baltimore harbor, withstood a two-day, massive bombardment by the British naval forces. Witnessing the action firsthand was Maryland lawyer, Francis Scott Key, who was aboard the Royal Navy ship, *HMS Tonnant*, negotiating the release of an American citizen, Dr. William Beanes. Key observed the British bombs and Congreve rockets hitting the fort all day on September 13, 1814 and subsequently throughout the night. Much to his delight, on the next day, he saw the fort's oversized stars and stripes garrison flag continue to wave. The Americans did not surrender the fort! Proud of his countrymen, Key wrote poignantly about the event in a poem, "Defence [*sic* "Defense] of Fort McHenry," that was subsequently set to music and eventually became the national anthem: *Star Spangled Banner*.

While the much-damaged Executive Mansion was being repaired and repainted, Mr. and Mrs. Madison moved into the Octagon House in the nation's capital on September 8, 1814. Coated in white paint, the building, at that point, began to be frequently called "The White House" (though it may have been called by some the "White House" earlier than 1814). On

November 2, Dolley reinstituted her weekly gatherings that were open to the public. Both her soirees and, unfortunately, the War of 1812 continued. The climactic end of the war was the Battle of New Orleans where the British sustained over 2,000 casualties beginning the week of January 8, 1815. The irony of this decisive battle is that a peace treaty was signed weeks *earlier* in Ghent, Belgium, on Christmas Eve, December 24, 1814. Due to the slow trans-Atlantic communications at the time, news of the peace treaty was too late for the belligerents to avoid the carnage that occurred at New Orleans. Nevertheless, this victory guaranteed a specific accomplishment. With this U.S. triumph, there was no longer any doubt as to who had complete dominion over the strategically vital Mississippi River and surrounding valleys. President Madison signed the Treaty of Ghent at the Octagon House on February 16, 1815. The War of 1812 ended with no readily *apparent* benefits derived by the Americans—no Canadian territory was conquered, no British armada was sunk. The Ghent Treaty did not even address the Royal Navy impressments of American seamen—the major reason for the war in the first place. Yet, the Americans attained from the war something far more invaluable. They proved to the world that the United States of America was indeed free and independent from British rule. The treaty also started a mutually beneficial peace between the British and the Americans that has lasted for over two centuries. The longest undefended border between any two countries is that between British America, now the independent country of Canada, and the U.S.A. The Madisons spent the summer of 1815—during peacetime rather than a year earlier amidst war--at their Montpelier home. Later that year, James and Dolley would return to Washington and take up residence at "The Seven Buildings" located at 1901 Pennsylvania Avenue. Here they would reside until the end of Madison's term of office on March 4, 1817.

Back to Montpelier

March 4, 1817 also marked the inauguration of James Monroe, the fifth President of the United States of America [see next essay].

Following the inauguration, the Madisons spent weeks attending "thank you" celebrations. Finally, James and Dolley returned to their splendid Montpelier estate. For the former president, now ailing, returning home was a well-earned respite from perennially draining government and wartime service. For Dolley, the change presented mixed emotions. Although she spent many years on farms in her youth, the rural tranquility of Montpelier necessitated a significant lifestyle adjustment. In spite of frequent guests visiting Montpelier, Dolley would deeply miss holding her weekly soirees at the Executive Mansion. On the other hand, in retirement, she relished having her "Great Little Madison" all to herself.

Dolley Madison in 1817.

However, not everything at Montpelier was gratifying to the former first couple. There were continual problems connected with Payne Todd. His alcoholism, errant behavior, and gambling debts were escalating beyond control. Dolley doted on her problematic son and gave him huge sums of money to pay off creditors. Likewise, the former president paid off Payne Todd's debts. All told, between 1813 and 1836, James Madison paid $30,000 to cover the arrears of this profligate individual. In spite of this substantial financial assistance, Payne Todd was twice forced into debtor's prison. Hard work, focus, and achievement were inherent character traits that James and Dolley demonstrated all their lives. These traits were entirely missing in this dissolute youth. Funds wasted covering Payne's debts, combined with substantial operating costs at Montpelier, presented daunting financial complications for the retired couple. Health issues were also problematic. Never robust, Madison's little remaining vitality began to wane in 1834, when he could no longer walk due to an advanced case of rheumatism. At this point, he was forced to spend the last two years of his life mostly in bed. With Dolley near, James Madison died on June 28, 1836, at 85 years of age. Dolley, now at age 68, was once again a widow. For the next 13 years, however, she would more than persevere--she would become an iconic figure in American history.

Dolley's Last Years and Legacy

Upon the death of James Madison, the Montpelier estate was left to Dolley. To pay off mounting debts, she began selling parts of the estate in 1837. However, these property sales did not generate enough funds to fully pay creditors. Adding to Dolley's troubles was her misguided decision to leave Payne Todd in charge of the estate after she moved back to Washington City. He was not only woefully incompetent, he also engaged in self-dealing, thereby further jeopardizing estate finances. In 1837, the U.S. Congress came to the aid of Dolley when the first three volumes of the James Madison papers were purchased for $30,000. Unfortunately, creditors seized much of these funds. Congress would subsequently purchase the remaining James Madison papers in May 1848. The agreement stipulated an upfront payment of $5,000 and the receipt of accrued annual interest from a $20,000 trust fund set up and accessible only by Dolley. This restriction in the new agreement was made to avoid seizure by Payne Todd's creditors. Dolley and Anna Coles Payne, the daughter of her younger brother John Coles Payne, lived together from late 1837 until Dolley's death in 1849. Dolley and her niece, Anna, moved back and forth between Montpelier and Washington. In the beginning of 1839, Dolley became active in the social life of the nation's capital. Famous on her own, she was also connected to then President Martin Van Buren through his eldest son's marriage to Dolley's cousin, Sarah

Angelica Singleton Van Buren. From late 1839 through most of 1841, Dolley stayed at Montpelier. In November 1841, she returned to Washington City. Except for an April 1842 visit to see friends in Philadelphia, and to secure a mortgage loan from New-York City financier John Jacob Astor, Dolley stayed in Washington City until September 1842 when she returned to Montpelier. After staying fifteen months there, she once again lived in Washington City. Unable to pay off outstanding debts, Dolley was finally forced to sell Montpelier to Richmond merchant Henry Wood Moncure in 1844. From then on, she and her niece, Anna, were living in the Richard Cutts House located within walking distance of the White House. Dolley continued to be invited to many official functions held at the nation's capital. In several photographs taken of her in the 1840s, she is seen wearing the same outfit, a black formal dress adorned with white scarf and white turban. One wonders about her clothes in these photos. Though still radiant in old age, Dolley is seen wearing the same outfit in nearly all these photos. Why? The obvious answer is that she was financially strapped and could not afford newer clothing. Dolley Madison biographer Holly C. Shulman provides an additional explanation. Dolley wore the same clothes as homage to an earlier time when she was the proud and vivacious First Lady of the United States of America.

Anna Coles Payne was with Dolley on July 12, 1849 when her aunt passed away. The next year, Anna married Dr. James H. Causten. Regrettably, this union would last only two years because Anna died in 1852. Earlier that year, on January 16, John Payne Todd had also passed away. Dolley Madison has justly earned a notable place in American history. The election for President of the United States in 1808 ended with Madison the winner. Federalist Party candidate, South Carolina Governor Charles Cotesworth Pinckney, conceded that: "I was beaten by Mr. and Mrs. Madison. I might have had a better chance had I faced Mr. Madison alone." This quote helps describe the effect and charismatic "soft" power Dolley had on the nation.

Portrait of Dolley Madison in her later years
(Property of the New-York Historical Society,
New York, NY).

At the dawn of the nineteenth century, and for 16 years thereafter, her accomplishments helped shape the role of First Lady. Dolley's trademark vitality and epoch-making effect on American history are acknowledged in publications written about her and her "Great Little Madison." Hugh Howard's 2012 biography, *Mr. and Mrs. Madison's War: America's First Couple and the Second War of Independence*, is just one of many examples where Dolley's extraordinary achievements are highlighted and recognized. The First Lady's courage and good sense in saving Stuart's portrait of Washington, not to mention her stalwart perseverance in helping the nation return to normalcy after Washington City was burned, have become hallmarks of her permanent legacy. During her time, women could not vote, let alone hold political office. Yet, through her extraordinary abilities, Dolley was able to effectively use charismatic power to positive and substantial effect. However, charisma alone would not have enabled the successes she attained. Dolley also had within her extraordinary courage and perseverance. She viewed herself as "the Mother of the Nation."

References:

(http://www.biography.com/people/dolley-madison-9394952; Retrieved 2/29/2016).

Côté, R. N. (2005). *Strength and Honor: The Life of Dolley Madison*. Corinthian Books.

Dolley Madison: America's First Lady. (2010). American Experience (TV program).

Howard, H. (2012). *Mr. and Mrs. Madison's War: America's First Couple and the Second War for Independence*. Bloomsbury Press.

Shulman, H. C. (2007). *Dolley Madison's Life and Times*. The University of Virginia Press.

Chapter 5
Elizabeth Kortright Monroe:
La Belle Américain Saves Adrienne de La Fayette During the French Revolution

In 1786, while a U.S. Congressman representing northern Virginia in the nation's temporary capital at New-York City, James Monroe met and fell instantly in love with 17 year-old Elizabeth Kortright. Capable and vivacious, Elizabeth came from a family who could trace their ethnic background to the Dutch settlers of *Nieuw Amsterdam* that later would become New-York City. James and Elizabeth were married in February 1786 and honeymooned on Long Island—at the time a bucolic, heavily forested isle surrounded by Long Island Sound to the north and the Atlantic Ocean to the east and south. One of James's highly envious friends commented: "Monroe d'camped for Long Island with the little smiling Venus in his Arms." A portrait of Elizabeth that captures the essence of that remark is displayed at their "Highland" home, which abuts Jefferson's Monticello estate in Charlottesville, Virginia.

Portrait of Elizabeth Kortright Monroe, aged 26, painted by Swiss artist Louis Sene in Paris (1794). (Property of Ash Lawn-Highland, Home of James and Elizabeth Monroe, Charlottesville, Virginia.)

James and Elizabeth Monroe, along with young daughter Eliza, arrived in chaotic Paris just three days following a *coup d'état* that resulted in the executions of "Reign of Terror" leaders Maximilien Robespierre, Louis Antoine de Saint-Just, and other members of the radical click known as the Jacobin Club. The turbulent French country was in the final days of the horrific "Reign of Terror" and entering into the next stage of its galvanic revolution known as the Thermidorean Period. In 1794, facing deadly insurrectionists, Elizabeth Monroe rode in a carriage marked as belonging to the U.S. Minister to France to check on the condition of Marie Adrienne Françoise de Noailles, wife of American military general Marquis de La Fayette. The French noblewoman was being held awaiting the same fate--the guillotine--that already claimed her sister, mother, and grandmother. As Elizabeth ventured into turbulent Paris streets, she was repeatedly surrounded by bloodthirsty mobs. Elizabeth boldly announced that she was the wife of the U.S. Minister to France and was seeking the release of a fellow American. Her visit to doomed Adrienne de La Fayette altered the opinion of the French *citoyens* resulting in the French noblewoman's release on January 22, 1795. For another 30 years, James Monroe would rise in his political career that culminated in eight years as U.S. president. Elizabeth was unquestionably devoted to him—and he to her. She supported him through successes and setbacks. Elizabeth was known for her exceptional beauty and elegance. In the last two decades of her life, she became afflicted with several illnesses—one of which may have been epilepsy. When she was incapacitated, Elizabeth asked her daughter Eliza Monroe Hay to substitute as First Lady. As Eliza's haughty manner proved to be unsuited for these tasks, Elizabeth was obligated to resume First Lady duties, whether she felt well or not. For her bravery in Paris and for coping with serious illness while supporting her husband, Elizabeth Monroe was an American hero.

James and Elizabeth Monroe—Early Lives

The future President and First Lady came from differing ethnic and regional backgrounds. James was from a gentrified Old Dominion family. His father, Spence Monroe, was of Scottish heritage and his mother, Elizabeth Jones Monroe, was of Welsh heritage. As were many Virginia planters, Monroe was "land rich but cash poor." He was raised in the Anglican Church that subsequently became the American Episcopal Church. Born in Westmoreland County, on April 28, 1758, Monroe entered the College of William and Mary in 1774. A year later, on April 19, 1775, the Minutemen of Massachusetts and the British Army fired on each other at Lexington and Concord igniting the War for Independence. At barely 18 years of age, Monroe joined the Continental Army as a lieutenant. At the pivotal Battle of Trenton, on December 26, 1776, Lieutenant Monroe received a wound in his chest from a bullet that passed into his left shoulder severing an artery. Nearly bleeding to death, James Monroe was saved by Dr. John Riker, a New Jersey surgeon who supported the "American Cause."

German artist Emmanuel Gottlieb Leutze's 1851 painting, "Washington Crossing the Delaware," located in the collection of the Metropolitan Museum of Art, New York, NY. Eighteen-year old Lieutenant James Monroe is standing behind Washington holding the 13-star U.S. Flag.

The young Virginian survived his battle wound and was then promoted to Captain. During the war, Monroe fought in key battles including those that took place at Harlem Heights, Brandywine, Germantown, and Monmouth. During the harsh winter encampment at Valley Forge in 1778, 19-year old Major Monroe shared a tent with fellow Virginian, Lieutenant John Marshall, later the Chief Justice of the U.S. Supreme Court. In 1780, Virginia Governor Thomas Jefferson promoted Monroe to a full colonelcy in the Virginia militia. He was also simultaneously appointed Virginia Military Commissioner to the Southern Continental Army. Three years later, Monroe was elected to the Virginia House of Delegates. As a member of this legislative body, he represented Virginia in the Continental Congress sessions from 1783 through 1786.

In early 1786, while serving as a U.S. Congressman in the nation's temporary capital in New-York City, Monroe was introduced to Elizabeth Kortright. She came from a Dutch New-York City family. Her many generations earlier forebear was *Bastian Van Kortryk*, who emigrated from The Netherlands to British Colonial America. Elizabeth's father, Lawrence Kortright, became wealthy from being a privateer during the French and Indian War. Although he took no part in the Revolutionary War, Kortright's sizable fortune from international trade was negatively impacted after the war when many former business associates shunned him for his loyalty to the Crown. James Monroe wrote to friend Thomas Jefferson in 1786 that Elizabeth was a daughter of a gentleman "injured in his fortunes." Nevertheless, the Kortright family was still well off financially. Elizabeth was born on June 30, 1768 and christened in the Dutch Reform Church. Exceptionally bright, Elizabeth received a formal education—a rarity for women during her time--and excelled in playing the pianoforte. At just five feet in height, Elizabeth possessed expressive blue eyes and a beautiful face enhanced by sumptuous brunette hair. James, ten years older than Elizabeth, was immediately smitten with this comely, petite 17-year old New-York City Dutch girl. After a brief courtship, they married on February 16, 1786 at Trinity Church, an Episcopal place of worship situated at the northern end of bustling Wall Street. This centuries-old church is still operational at its original site, which happens to be one block from the original World Trade Center that was destroyed on September 11, 2001. Resurrected, the gleaming new structure, obstinately taller than the original at 1776 feet in height, proudly bears the name: "One World Trade Center."

Trinity Church (left) about the time of the Monroe marriage;
Trinity Church with the original World Trade Center in the background.

One World Trade Center was completed on May 13, 2013. The new structure was erected on the site of the original World Trade Center that was destroyed when commandeered jetliners crashed into the Twin Towers on September 11, 2001. The gleaming new "One World Trade Center," also known as "The Freedom Tower," is obstinately taller than the original WTC at 1776 feet. It is by far the tallest structure in the Western Hemisphere.

The newlyweds lived in a large Manhattan manse with Elizabeth's widowed father (Elizabeth's mother Hannah Aspinwall passed away in 1777. The Aspinwall family is directly related to the Roosevelts of Hyde Park, NY. President Franklin Delano Roosevelt's youngest son was named John Aspinwall Roosevelt). As soon as his term as Congressman ended, James Monroe planned to bring his new bride to Virginia and earn a living as an attorney. By fall 1786, Elizabeth was pregnant and loath to leave her father. In a letter to Thomas Jefferson, Monroe wrote: "She left her state and her family and became a good Virginian." With a reputation as a Continental Army war hero, and with close connections to Jefferson, Madison, and Washington, Monroe quickly established a law practice with many clients. A great number of them, like he, were "land rich but cash poor." In April 1787, voters in Fredericksburg elected him to the Virginia Assembly in Richmond. A shortage of money was an issue. Monroe lacked funds to bring his wife and daughter with him while serving on the Virginia Circuit Court. Devoted to his family, he compensated for these frequent separations by returning to his Fredericksburg home as often as possible. Monroe was thrilled to be a member of the Virginia Assembly. This was especially true during the December 1787 legislative debate over ratification of the newly inked "Constitution of the United States of America." The debate over ratification in Virginia included two formidable orators: John Marshall and Patrick Henry. Marshall spoke strongly in favor of ratification. Henry, known as the "Cicero of the South" for his fiery and persuasive oratory, argued against ratification. Monroe voted with Henry against ratification. However, the Virginia Assembly, as a whole, voted in favor of ratifying the U.S. Constitution.

Embodied within the document is the structure of the bicameral legislative branch of the federal government consisting of the Senate and the House of Representatives. James Madison and Monroe ran against each other in the first U.S. congressional election representing northern Virginia. Though Madison won, the two remained friends. In a situation where "one door closes and another opens," an unfortunate death in Monroe's extended family created an opportunity. William Grayson, Monroe's cousin, was elected to the U.S. Senate in 1788 and served from March 4, 1789 until his sudden death from a heart attack on March 12, 1790. Grayson was the first person to die while serving in an elective office of the newly formed U.S. government. Grayson's death created a potential opportunity for Monroe, who submitted his name to the Virginia legislature for filling Grayson's now vacant Senate seat. In fall 1790, the Virginian legislature voted its approval for Monroe to complete Grayson's senate term. The 32-year old lawyer was sworn-in as U.S. Senator on December 6, 1790. James could now—gladly—put his legal career on hold.

James Monroe in his early career.

The Federal government at this time was located in Philadelphia. Elizabeth would frequently travel 90 miles to New-York City to care for her father who was now ill. By this time, Jefferson, Madison, and Monroe were leading a political movement deeply opposed to Federalist policies. These breakaway anti-Federalist politicians were called "Jeffersonian Republicans," and the political body they formed was called the Republican Party. Beginning in 1799, the political entity was renamed the Democratic-Republican Party. During the Jacksonian Era, the political unit became and remains the Democratic Party.

The Monroes in Paris

There was the belief, especially in the idealistic concepts of individuals such as Jefferson and Monroe, that the French Revolution would follow the American Revolution paradigm. In this vision, the oppressed French people would peacefully overthrow the unpopular Bourbon monarchy and form a democracy. This did not occur in France. In July 1789, a rebellion commenced that lasted a decade and resulted in the deaths by guillotine of the reigning French king and queen. The revolution in France quickly devolved into a steady stream of mass murder that has been estimated to exceed 41,000 victims. In September 1789, Jefferson vacated his post as U.S. Minister to France. Though Jefferson expected to return to France, newly elected President George Washington had another role for the author of the Declaration of Independence. Washington wanted Jefferson to serve as the first U.S. Secretary of State. In filling the vacant post of U.S. Minister to France, Washington proposed that a Federalist colleague, Gouveneur Morris, fill this position. Morris was of Dutch New-York City heritage similar to that of Elizabeth Kortright. However, whereas she loved the French and their culture, Morris did not and was stridently pro-British. The Republicans, at this time a minority faction in the U.S. Senate, were pro-French and voiced strong opposition to Morris based on his monarchical political leanings. On January 12, 1792, the Federalist majority in the Senate approved Morris as U.S. Minister to France. After his appointment, Morris did not tone down his ultraconservative rhetoric. He publicly denounced the 1793 executions of French King Louis XVI and Queen Marie Antoinette. By 1794, the insurrectionists gained control of the beleaguered French government. One of their first actions was to demand the recall of Morris. The native New-Yorker had no wish to remain in chaotic France and hurriedly evacuated his post.

President Washington then offered the U.S. Minister to France post to James Monroe. The Monroe couple and seven-year old Eliza sailed to France and landed at the English Channel port of Le Havre on July 31, 1794. Here they heard the shocking news that three days earlier Maximilien Robespierre, Louis Antoine de Saint-Just, and other leaders of the radical click known as the Jacobin Club that fostered the "Reign of Terror" were beheaded.

A French insurrectionist holding a severed head of someone who had just been guillotined during the "Reign of Terror."

Following the demise of these murderous dictators, the French *citoyens* formed a broader-based governing body called: *Le Convention*. The French were at first suspicious of the newly arrived U.S. Minister based on their previous disdain for Morris. Unlike the pro-British Federalist, the Virginia lawyer, who helped establish the 18th century Republican Party, was ardently pro-French. Monroe's beautiful wife, fluent in *le français*, was quickly soon adored by the French public. James and Elizabeth sent Eliza to a French finishing school run by Madame Campan in St. Germain-en-Laye, a Paris suburb. Here Eliza was inculcated in the manners and polish of the *ancien régime*. According to Monroe biographer Harry Ammon (1990): "Unfortunately, this aristocratic polish was accompanied by a large measure of snobbery. Her pupils, including Eliza Monroe, tended to develop exaggerated notions of their own importance, whatever their origins. Eliza, at this time an only child much indulged by her parents, emerged from Mme. Campan's school a vain young lady who never forgot (and gladly reminded all and sundry) that Hortense de Beauharnais had been a friend of her schooldays. Such open snobbery made her highly unpopular with her contemporaries." Eliza's schoolmate later became the wife of Napoleon Bonaparte's brother, Louis, King of Holland, and the mother of Napoleon III, Emperor of the French. Years later when she was married to George Hay, Eliza named her daughter "Hortensia" after her illustrious friend. Unfortunately, Eliza would affect a similar regal attitude when she substituted for her ailing mother, Elizabeth, as First Lady. In doing so, Eliza engendered enmity toward the Monroes, especially Elizabeth.

La Belle Américaine: American Hero

With Monroe and his French-speaking wife captivated with France, a growing comity developed between the U.S.A. and its closest ally during the Revolutionary War. Twenty-six year-old Elizabeth was adored by Parisians who named her: *La Belle*

Américaine. Beautiful, Elizabeth was also courageous. In 1794, the frail wife of Gilbert du Motier, Marquis de La Fayette, was imprisoned in a Paris jail. Madame Marie Adrienne Françoise de Noailles, Marquise de La Fayette, was from noble birth. Members of the French nobility were now facing the guillotine in France. Awaiting the fate that befell her sister, mother, and grandmother, Adrienne had given up hope of being rescued. Adrienne's uncle, diplomat Emmanuel Marie Louis de Noailles, asked Monroe to help Adrienne. As an American official, James Monroe considered it his duty to obtain the release of the wife of Marquis de La Fayette, who wore a Continental Army general's uniform and bravely fought in the War for Independence. However, Monroe feared that intervening directly in her release would cause an international incident. So Monroe devised an indirect plan for her rescue. The Americans would demonstrate to the French that Adrienne, wife of a former American general, was under the protection of the U.S.A. In his autobiography, James Monroe states that he "procured a carriage of his own as soon as he could, had it put in the best order, and his servants dressed in like manner. In this carriage Mrs. Monroe drove directly to the prison in which Madame Lafayette was confined." The individual who was to actually carry out this scheme faced enormous risk. Elizabeth volunteered to undertake this dangerous task. Accompanied only by two servants, *La Belle Américaine* went to the prison where Adrienne was being held. She rode in a carriage through deadly Paris crowds that were primed to murder anyone they so wished. Monroe writes further in his autobiography: "In this carriage Mrs. Monroe drove directly to the prison. Inquiry was made, whose carriage was it? The answer given was that of the American Minister. Who is in it? His wife. What brought her here? To see Madame Lafayette." When the mobs were told that in the carriage was the wife of the popular U.S. Minister to France on her way to see Adrienne, Mrs. Monroe was permitted to proceed.

American hero, future First Lady Elizabeth Kortright Monroe, rescued Madame Marie Adrienne Françoise de Noailles, Marquise de La Fayette, from execution.

Elizabeth Monroe's presence at the prison to aid her "fellow American" swayed public opinion. In response to calls to free Adrienne, the French Committee of Public Safety was forced to release the French noblewoman from prison on January 22, 1795. In risking her life in order to save Adrienne, Marquise de La Fayette, Elizabeth Kortright Monroe certainly qualifies as an American hero!

Departure from and then Encore Return to France

On July 4, 1796, U.S. Minister to France, James Monroe, celebrated his country's 20th birthday in Paris amidst much symbolic celebration and fanfare. When it was time for toast making, Monroe honored President George Washington. The audience at the celebration, no doubt a good number of which were intoxicated, consisted of members of opposing American political parties: the Federalists and the anti-Federalists Republicans. Following Monroe's toast to the U.S. president, Republicans shouted insults at the Founding Father. The Federalists responded in kind, and a scuffle ensued that soon led into a full-fledged brawl. Word of the riot in Paris reached President Washington, who was already becoming displeased with Monroe for being too pro-French. Washington favored staunch American neutrality between France and Great Britain. When news of the Paris brawl was publicized in American newspapers, Vice President John Adams wrote that Monroe was "a disgraced minister" who had insulted "the government of my country." Though Monroe neither instigated nor participated in the Paris riot, he nevertheless was held responsible for this embarrassing event. Shortly thereafter, Monroe was recalled as Minister to France. The riot served as a ready excuse for recalling Monroe, a founder of the 18th century Republican Party, which ardently opposed Federalist policies, many of which were originally formulated and promoted by Alexander Hamilton.

Returning from France, the Monroe family arrived in Philadelphia on June 27, 1797. The "City of Brotherly Love" did not live up to its nickname by offering James Monroe an at-best lukewarm welcome. Shortly thereafter, the Monroe family visited New- York City. The Monroes left Philadelphia sometime after July 25 for their Albermarle farm, which is now known as Monroe Hill on the grounds of the University of Virginia. Living near the founder of the university, Monroe often visited Jefferson, who became vice president when Adams ascended to the presidency. By late summer 1797, Monroe reluctantly resumed his legal career; but politics was still foremost on his mind. Monroe ran for and was elected governor of Virginia and served at the state capital in Richmond beginning in December 1799. Earlier that year in May, a son was born and named after James and James' father, Spence. Tragically, James Spence Monroe contracted whooping cough and died on September 28, 1800 leaving his parents and sister Eliza heartbroken. On his little gravestone there was only room to etch his initials: J.S.M. (It should be noted that there are inconsistencies in secondary reference sources regarding birth and death dates of the Monroe children. Helping to resolve these conflicting dates is Dan Preston at the University of Mary Washington. Preston is heading the research project cataloging James Monroe's papers and has uncovered documentation indicating the precise birth date, April 8, 1802, of the Monroes' third child named Maria Hester Monroe.) The end of 1802 signaled the conclusion of Monroe's third year as Virginia governor. For Monroe it was now a return to his law practice—but not for long.

On January 10, 1803, Monroe received an urgent note from President Jefferson "to join the resident Minister, Robert R. Livingston, in an effort to purchase a site at the mouth of the Mississippi to be used as a port of deposit" (Ammon, p.203). The third U.S. president desperately needed Monroe to accept the position of "Envoy Extraordinary to France and Spain." Rumors were circulating, later proven to be accurate, that Spain had ceded to France the Louisiana Territory, a vast extent of land the precise size of which was unknown at the time. With France continually at war with Great Britain and its European allies, *Général Napoléon* required additional cash to continue his conquests across the continent. As timing was critical, Jefferson pleaded with Monroe to immediately undertake the assignment and sail off to France. Prior to leaving the U.S., Jefferson gave Monroe specific instructions. The "Envoy Extraordinary to France and Spain" was to purchase, with a relatively free hand in terms of price, the port of New Orleans and secure navigation rights to the Mississippi River. Before sailing to France, the Monroes rode north to visit Kortright family members in New-York City. However, their stay in the city was extended due to bitter temperatures that froze New-York Bay. Finally, on March 8, 1803, the ice jam began to melt; and the Monroe family's departure to France soon commenced. Crossing the Atlantic in winter was always perilous. The winter of 1803 was especially harsh with ice storms and mountainous squalls that rendered all members of the Monroe family seasick. In addition, Elizabeth was being affected by rheumatism, an ailment that would plague her for the rest of her life. Fortunately, Elizabeth had 16-year old Eliza to help her tend to 11-month old Maria Hester.

<u>Louisiana Purchase and Assignment in London</u>

After their 29-day arduous journey, the Monroes arrived in the port of Le Havre on April 8, 1803 that was coincidentally Maria Hester's first birthday. They were welcomed with celebrations featuring numerous displays of French and American flags. Already in Paris awaiting Monroe's arrival was American

Ambassador to France, Robert R. Livingston (1746-1834), who had already begun negotiations with French Foreign Minister Charles Maurice de Talleyrand-Périgord. With a reputation for duplicity and underhandedness, Talleyrand was circumspect in his dealings with Livingston. Deliberations with Talleyrand over the land purchase were at a standstill. However, *Général Napoléon* critically needed money for his colossal army that was overrunning much of continental Europe. The soon-to-be *Empéror de France* assigned Marquis François de Barbé-Marbois to deal directly with Monroe. The American envoy was pleasantly surprised with the offer to purchase the entire Louisiana Territory. Monroe instantly accepted on behalf of his nation. In return for land area larger than France, Great Britain, Portugal, and Spain combined, the U.S. paid 80 million *francs* (the equivalent of $15,000,000) for 828,000 square miles of land. Stated another way, this came to approximately four cents per acre! While this was astounding in terms of size, Monroe's mission was still unfulfilled because he was also tasked to purchase West Florida from the Spanish. However, Monroe faced intractable resistance by the Spanish to sell their Florida territories.

In mid-1803, James Monroe was ordered to report to London. He expected to be shunned in London for his widely known anti-British sentiments. Much to his pleasant surprise, the British welcomed him and his family. The British also revealed to Monroe their pleasure in knowing that the Louisiana Territory was now out of the control of their centuries-old archenemy France. However, there were major problems festering between the two English-speaking nations. The most egregious issue was the forced impressments of Americans into the British Royal Navy. Though there were a small number of British deserters on American vessels, the bulk of the seamen impressed from American ships were indeed American citizens. There was also the "blown out of proportion" treatment of British Ambassador to the U.S., Anthony Merry, by President Jefferson. Upon presenting his credentials to Jefferson, Ambassador Merry was dressed in embroidered, formal attire. At their meeting, Merry claimed that Jefferson was wearing "farmer clothes and slippers." Jefferson insulted Merry further by not taking the hand of the British Ambassador's wife while filing into the dinner hall of the then-named Executive Mansion. Jefferson deliberately took Dolley Madison's hand instead. These affronts were relayed to London. Once news of Merry's impolite treatment by Jefferson reached Whitehall, the center of the British government, the Monroes were then correspondingly snubbed.

London weather was also distressing the Monroe family. The cold, smog-laden London air was adversely affecting Elizabeth's rheumatism. It was also hurting baby Maria Hester, who had respiratory trouble. In addition to having ill family members, Monroe desperately needed to leave London for Spain to fulfill his mission of obtaining West Florida. In selling vast territories to the Americans, the French made oral assurances that were not written into the actual documents of the land transfer. This led to disputes between Spain and the U.S.A. The French negotiators had given Monroe verbal assurances that Spain would readily sell sparsely populated West Florida to the Americans. When Monroe approached Spanish authorities in London regarding the purchase of this territory, he received a negative response. The Spanish argued that the purchase of the Louisiana Territories had no bearing whatsoever regarding West Florida.

Stymied diplomatically in London in acquiring West Florida from the Spanish, Monroe and his family returned to Paris. On December 2, 1804, James and Elizabeth Monroe attended the sumptuously staged coronation of *Napoléon Buonaparte* crowning himself *Napoléon I, Empereur de France*. Pope Pius VII, who was *abducted* to Paris for this event, was to ceremoniously crown the French ruler. However, conceited *Napoléon* crowned himself. A week later, Monroe, without family, set off to Spain first by ship and later by mule. With weapons loaded to ward off thieving brigands, Monroe finally arrived in Madrid on January 1, 1805. After months of fruitless negotiations, Monroe wrote to his immediate supervisor

Secretary of State Madison that the only way to attain West Florida was through military force. Madison deemed this to be impossible because congressional approval for going to war with Spain was unattainable. Monroe returned to Paris and his family in June 1805. Shortly thereafter, he reluctantly returned to London with family for continued negotiation attempts to end disputes between Great Britain and the U.S.A. Again, Monroe met intransigence by the British. Worse still, Elizabeth was beginning to faint from the onset of what has been speculated to be epilepsy.

Added to James' troubles were the actions of warring France and Great Britain. Both countries were fearful that the United States would take the opposing side in this war that was rapidly spreading across Europe. As a consequence, the navies of both countries were escalating the seizures of American cargo vessels. With overseas commerce crippled by these actions, the American economy began to falter. The U.S. response was the passing of the Non-Importation Act on October 28, 1806 that suppressed trade with Great Britain. A year later saw the imposition of the more draconian Embargo Act of 1807 that totally barred all trade with France as well as with Great Britain.

In his role as ""Envoy Extraordinary," Monroe tried tirelessly to resolve differences between the two English-speaking countries. The 1806 treaty that Monroe and U.S. Emissary to the British Parliament William Pinkney made with British representatives Lord Auckland and Lord Holland resolved some contentious issues, but did not end the policy of impressing American sailors. This London treaty was sent to President Jefferson. Failing to eliminate the most egregious problem between the countries, Jefferson rejected the Monroe-Pinkney Treaty and placed it in his desk drawer--and there it remained. In late June 1807, Secretary of State Madison recalled Monroe from his British ministerial post.

Recalled from his London assignment, Monroe and his family boarded the *USS Augustus* and set sail for America. Arriving in Norfolk, Virginia, Monroe immediately traveled to Washington

City to meet with Jefferson and Madison. Tacitly recognizing Monroe's service to America, the President and Secretary of State offered a polite but somewhat shallow "Thank You." Jefferson offered Monroe the position of Governor of the Louisiana Territory. Monroe politely declined the offer. His Virginia "friends" had no other job or task for him. Given this cold-shoulder treatment, Monroe left Washington City deeply hurt. Jefferson later wrote to Monroe explaining his actions. However, Monroe was still angry with Madison.

On a more positive and familial note, George Hay, a prominent Virginian attorney whose most famous case was the prosecution of Aaron Burr for treason, was a frequent caller at the Monroe "Highland" home. When Hay asked for Eliza's hand in marriage, the proud, self-confident young woman readily accepted. They were married in October 1808. On December 7, 1808, Madison easily won the election as the nation's fourth president. At the same time, Monroe had won a seat in the Virginia legislature. By the fall of this year, James and Elizabeth were expecting their first grandchild. In September 1809, the Monroes were ecstatic in welcoming Hortensia Monroe Hay to the family. Being elected again to the Virginia legislature and the joy of becoming a grandfather did not alleviate Monroe's anger towards Madison. Whether for cynical political reasons or simply to re-unite former colleagues, Jefferson made repeated efforts to rekindle the friendship between the two James. By 1810, this was accomplished.

<u>Monroe Becomes Secretary of State; Elizabeth becomes seriously ill</u>

In January 1811, with the death of a federal judge, Madison appointed Virginia Governor John Tyler to the vacant judgeship. Monroe was greatly admired for his diplomatic successes in Europe by members of the Virginia legislature, who readily elected him to complete the term of Tyler as Governor of Virginia. This was the fourth time Monroe was elected as Virginia Governor. Two months later, on March 20, 1811, President Madison wrote to

Monroe urging the newly installed governor of Virginia to resign and accept the position of U.S. Secretary of State. Madison was having great difficulties with his Secretary of State Robert Smith. Madison and Smith disagreed vociferously on a range of foreign policy matters. In Madison's March 20 communiqué, the fourth U.S. president wrote: "I am more anxious to hear from you as soon as possible, since…the business of the [State] Department is…peculiarly urgent as well as important." Monroe accepted but cautioned Madison that he would be asserting his prerogative as the most important cabinet member. Furthermore, Monroe had just been elected governor of Virginia. For him to vacate this office so soon would require an open letter to the Virginia legislature from Madison explaining why Monroe had to leave the governorship. This did not quite happen. Instead, Madison wrote a lengthy letter directly to Monroe emphasizing the latter's outstanding skills as a negotiator and emissary. He also stated bluntly that the U.S.A. faced a national emergency that required someone as able as Monroe. An elated and vindicated Monroe wrote back: "The just principles on which you have invited me into the department of State have removed every difficulty which had occurred to me." Upon receiving Monroe's reply, Madison was relieved to find a capable replacement for Smith.

Within weeks of assuming the position of U.S. Secretary of State, Monroe launched verbal attacks against the British and French who were still at war. Both nations were seizing American cargo ships. The French acquiesced to Monroe by releasing American ships trapped in French ports. However, the British seemed intent on going to war by continuing the seizures of American sailors and ships. Adding to Monroe's problems at his new post was a family crisis. Elizabeth was experiencing mounting health ailments, which James described as "indisposition." Ill to the point of being incapacitated, Elizabeth requested that Eliza assume some of the social duties required of the wife of the U.S. Secretary of State. Unfortunately, Eliza was not well suited for this task. She repeatedly displayed haughtiness that offended members of

Washington City's social milieu.

The War of 1812

By 1812, America was divided by political party affiliation. The Democrat-Republicans had strongholds in the U.S. south, west, and in cities nationwide with burgeoning immigrant populations such as New-York City, Philadelphia, and Baltimore. Voters favoring the Federalist Party were shrinking in number and confined for the most part to the New England states. The Federalists favored continued trade with Great Britain and were adamantly opposed to war with the former "Mother Country." However, the Democrat-Republicans favored expanding the power and size of the nation embodied in the notion later dubbed "Manifest Destiny." The most extreme party members were called "War Hawks" led by Henry Clay, Sr. of Kentucky, who were pushing for war with Great Britain. After negotiations with the British failed, President Madison went to the U.S. Congress on April 1, 1812 and obtained a 60-day reinstatement of a complete trade embargo with that nation. In quelling rapidly worsening relations with the U.S.A., the British Parliament voted to end the impressments of American sailors on June 23, 1812. It was too little, too late. Five days earlier, at Madison's urging, Congress declared war on Great Britain. The U.S.A. at this time had a diminutive standing army and a navy that was pitifully smaller than that possessed by the British Crown. By spring 1813, British ships were blockading Charleston, New-York City, Point Royal, and Savannah as well as the mouth of the Mississippi River that flows into New Orleans. Madison appointed Brigadier General John Armstrong, of Pennsylvania, as Secretary of War to defend the nation.

Though the U.S. Navy won several key battles at sea, the American armies, composed mainly of state militias, were almost always routed with catastrophic casualties. Secretary of State Monroe suggested to Armstrong that he strengthen land and naval forces defending Washington City. Armstrong refused arguing that the threat of a raid on the nation's capital to be only a strategic ruse by the British, who were far more inclined in fending off American incursions into Canada. The Americans *did* invade Canada several times and burnt much of York—today's Toronto. However, these American raids into Canada were irresponsibly misguided in purpose and resulted in complete failures. Monroe at this time received a message from U.S. Minister to Russia John Quincy Adams relaying the Czar's offer to negotiate peace with Great Britain. President Madison declined the Czar's offer. However, he readily acceded to the Crown authorities' offer to begin peace negotiations at the Belgium city of Ghent beginning in November 1813. Madison sent emissaries for this purpose. However, circumstances changed. After suffering major battlefield losses, *Napoléon I* was forced to sign the April 11, 1814 Treaty of Fontainebleau, which ended his tenure as French emperor and exiled him to Elba. The powerful Britain military was now free from the European conflict to fight the Americans and perhaps regain lost colonies.

Considering the monumental threat to the nation, Secretary of War Armstrong shockingly neglected the defense of Washington City. On May 3, 1813, the British armada attacked at the north Chesapeake Bay village of Havre de Grace, Maryland. Fifteen months later, on August 18, 1914, the British landed a major invasion force at Benedict, Maryland. Shortly thereafter, the Americans put up substantial resistance but were overwhelmed at the Battle of Bladensburg on August 24. As Monroe incisively predicted, Washington City was indeed the target for invasion. Within hours, the British were torching many government buildings, including the Executive Mansion. Fortunately, overnight a massive thunderstorm combined with deadly winds disrupted the British marauders. The heavy torrents of rain thankfully doused raging fires in buildings preventing many from being burnt to the ground. Nineteen days later, on September 13, the British launched a multipronged attack on Baltimore and nearby villages. Unlike at the nation's capital city, the British met effective, deadly land forces at North Point, five miles before Baltimore. The British also faced massive earthworks and 100 cannons at Hampstead Hill. However, it was

Fort McHenry that was the strongest and most strategic defense of the city. Situated to guard Baltimore harbor, Fort McHenry was a substantial military installation in the shape of a multi-pointed star. On September 13, 1814, the British began an all-out bombardment of the fort that lasted for 25 hours. On the morning of September 14, the British observed a giant garrison flag being raised over the fort. The flag sent an unambiguous signal to the British that the Americans would continue an unyielding defense of the fort as well as Baltimore. This huge garrison flag was hand sewn by Mary Young Pickersgill. This flag is the iconic "Star Spangled Banner," a patriotic and apt symbol of American tenacity.

On September 14, British ships began departing from Chesapeake Bay. Also on this date, President Madison appointed James Monroe as the replacement for dishonored Secretary of War John Armstrong. Now James Monroe wore two hats: Secretary of State and Secretary of War. With these enormous responsibilities placed before him, Monroe feared that his nation was woefully unprepared to fight the British. Therefore, he drew up a plan to build a standing army of 100,000 soldiers in the defense of the country. Thankfully, the war was coming to an end. The "War of 1812" officially ended on Christmas Eve, December 24, 1814 at the Belgium city of Ghent. However, news of the signing of the Treaty of Ghent occurred after General Andrew Jackson heroically led an array of Americans from a polyglot of ethnic, racial, and religious backgrounds that decimated the British army at the Battle of New Orleans in January 1815. On February 18, the U.S. Senate ratified the treaty. The U.S.A. gained no new territories in the war. However, the nation attained something far more important. It proved that it could ably defend itself against the world's greatest army and navy!

Monroe Becomes President; Elizabeth becomes Incapacitated

On March 4, 1817, Monroe was inaugurated fifth U.S. president. During the first years of the Monroe Administration, the nation remained at peace with a minimum of partisan turmoil. The

Virginian, who was labeled "Last of the Cocked Hats," "Last of the Founding Fathers," and "Last of the Virginia Dynasty," visited Boston in July 1817. Federalist-leaning journalist and publisher Benjamin Russell wrote in the *Columbian Sentinel* on July 12 that the nation was at peace and united. Russell said the U.S.A. was entering an "Era of Good Feelings." During Monroe's time in office, the nation continued to expand its land area. Spanish Minister Luis de Onís y Gonzales-Vara and Secretary of State John Quincy Adams reached an agreement whereby Spain ceded its Florida territories to the U.S.A., and at the same time established the western U.S. boundary with Spanish-held territory.

However, much of the "Era of Good Feelings" euphoria ended with the "Panic of 1819" that lasted for two years. In 1820, Monroe signed into law the "Missouri Compromise." With this critically important agreement, the nation defused the threat of war between the "North" and the "South" over the accursed "peculiar institution of slavery." Americans were also flexing power on a global basis. Based on a principle that the European powers must not interfere in the Western Hemisphere and the U.S.A. must not become entangled in European disputes, Monroe adopted a document prepared by Secretary of State John Quincy Adams. On December 2, 1823, President Monroe recited this document within his address to Congress. Monroe declared that the U.S.A. would hereby protect the newly independent, former colonies of Spain against any aggression by European powers. About two decades following the death of James Monroe in 1831, this landmark principle of a hemispheric shield of protection became known as the "Monroe Doctrine."

While James was achieving major success in his presidency, Elizabeth was suffering from progressively worsening illnesses. Elizabeth, now in her fifties, attempted to fulfill her First Lady responsibilities. However, she could not match the social élan and verve of her celebrated predecessor Dolley Madison. Cokie Roberts, in *Ladies of Liberty: The Women Who Shaped Our Nation*, concurs: "Elizabeth Monroe was no Dolley Madison, who would be an impossible act to follow" (p. 319). Whereas Dolley would doff elaborately feathered, turbaned hats and joyously intermingle with constituents, senate wives, and foreign diplomats, Elizabeth was more restrained in her dealings with guests in the newly repaired Executive Mansion. Unable to participate in some social functions due to illness, Elizabeth's absence was inaccurately linked to her being aloof and detached. Daughter Eliza added to her mother's problems when she substituted as First Lady. Schooled in Europe and taught by Madame Campan, a staunch believer in aristocratic manners, Eliza offended White House guests. Along with being condescending, Eliza was also controlling. Maria Hester was deeply hurt by Eliza who autocratically limited the invitation list for her younger sister's wedding in the Executive Mansion, later to be called the White House.

For some misguided reason, Eliza did not want politicians and, most especially, foreign diplomats to attend the wedding of her 17-year old sister, Maria Hester, to Samuel Lawrence Gouveneur on March 9, 1820. The New-York City-born lawyer was Monroe's nephew and also served as the president's private secretary. Eliza's actions spoiled Maria Hester's wedding, the first event of its kind in the White House for a sitting president. Louisa Catherine Johnson Adams, the European-raised American wife of then Secretary of State John Quincy Adams and herself a future First Lady, referred to Eliza in her diary as being "so proud and so mean I scarcely ever met such a compound." With her dictatorial actions, Eliza not only embittered her sister but also tarnished the legacy of Elizabeth Monroe as First Lady. This is unfortunate because it undermines Elizabeth's bravery in France. She was instrumental in saving the life of Adrienne de La Fayette. For her courage in facing down Paris mobs and for her unwavering support to her husband while he served in a wide array of elected and appointed positions during a political career that spanned four decades, Elizabeth was a heroic, most worthy First Lady.

Portraits of Elizabeth and James Monroe
during the Monroe Presidential Administration.

Portraits of the Monroe daughters:
Eliza Monroe Hay and
Maria Hester Monroe Gouveneur.

James and Elizabeth Monroe: The Final Years

On New Year's Day in 1825, James and Elizabeth Monroe held their last major "levee" in the White House. Elizabeth's appearance at this event has been described as follows: "Her dress was superb black; neck and arms bare and beautifully formed; her hair in puffs and dressed high on the head and ornamented with white ostrich plumes; around her neck an elegant necklace. Though no longer young, she is still a very handsome woman." After James Monroe ended his second term as president, the couple again faced financial troubles. As a consequence, they were forced to sell their Highland home in Albemarle County. They retired to their Oak Hill home in Aldie, Virginia. On December 29, 1826, James Monroe wrote to nephew and son-in-law Samuel L. Gouveneur from his Oak Hill home that Elizabeth "had a convulsion, which was attended with the most painful consequences" (quote provided by Ms. Nancy Stetz, Education Program Manager at Ash Lawn Highland). After Elizabeth awoke from this seizure, she was burned over many areas of her body.

Further tragedies would follow four years later. Daughter Eliza's husband, George Hay, born on December 17, 1765 died on September 21, 1830 at the age of 64. During late summer 1830, Elizabeth was gravely ill. After a brief recovery, her health worsened and she died on September 23 at age 62. James was devastated by the loss of his wife of 44 years. Following Elizabeth's death, the former president moved in with daughter Maria Hester Monroe Gouveneur and her husband in the same municipality where Elizabeth was born: New-York City. After Elizabeth died, James told family and friends that he would not live long. His ominous prediction proved true, for he died less than 10 months after his "little smiling Venus." At age 73, James Monroe died on July 4, 1831—exactly 55 years to the day after the signing of the Declaration of Independence. For their many significant contributions to the nation, James and Elizabeth Monroe should always be remembered and thanked!

Note: Much appreciation to Ms. Nancy Stetz, Education Program Manager, Ash Lawn-Highland, Charlottesville, Virginia, home of James and Elizabeth Monroe, for her extensive assistance!

References:

Ammon, H. (1990). *James Monroe: The Quest for National Identity*. University of Virginia Press.

Black, A. (2009). *The First Ladies of the United States of America*. The White House Historical Association.

Roberts, C. (2008). *Ladies of Liberty: The Women Who Shaped Our Nation*. William Morrow.

Chapter 6
USN "Airdales" in the Pacific Theater of World War II / USN Air Crewman Wings

The Japanese attack on American military installations at Pearl Harbor was devastating. As a result of the December 7, 1941 attack: the U.S. Navy and Marine Corps suffered a total of 2,896 casualties of whom 2,117 were deaths (Navy 2,008, Marines 109) and 779 wounded (Navy 710, Marines 69). The U.S. Army as of midnight, December 10, lost 228. In addition, at least 57 civilians were killed and nearly as many seriously injured. (http://worldwar2history.info/Pearl-Harbor/; Retrieved 2/29/2016.)

Eight U.S. Navy battleships were severely damaged—four of which were sunk--at the sneak attack on December 7, 1941 at Pearl Harbor.
USN aircraft staged on a carrier called a "flattop."

The U.S. Navy lost 21 ships that were badly damaged or sunk—eight of which were battleships. A total of 350 land-based aircraft were also destroyed. Providentially, the American "flattop" aircraft carriers were at the time out at sea and thus spared to fight another day. *And did they!* The naval war in the Pacific Ocean involved ships often battling sometimes hundreds of miles away from each other. The opposing American and Japanese navies dueled with carrier-based aircraft. The first significant aerial battle between American and Japanese carrier aircraft occurred during the planned attack on the *USS Lexington*.

"Butch" O'Hare's Valor and the Naming of America's Busiest Airport

In April 1942, USN Lieutenant Edward Henry "Butch" O'Hare and his wingman flying F4F Wildcats eyed a formation of nine Japanese heavy bombers targeting their aircraft carrier, the *USS Lexington*. O'Hare and his wingman dove at the bombers. However, his wingman had engine trouble and was forced to return to *"The Lex."* This did not deter O'Hare. Through outstanding "dog fighting" and with much bravery, O'Hare shot down five bombers before running out of ammunition. By then, the rest of his squadron joined in the mêlée; and the remaining four bombers were destroyed. O'Hare was immediately promoted to Lieutenant Commander and became the U.S. Navy's first "Flying Ace" of WWII. For his valor, he was awarded the U.S. Congressional Medal of Honor. Just over a year and a half later, on November 26, 1943, while piloting a F6F Grumman Hellcat in another dogfight with Japanese bombers, O'Hare was shot down and killed. In 1949, Chicago's Orchard Airfield was renamed, in his honor, O'Hare International Airport--America's busiest in terms of aircraft traffic.

Photographs of U.S. Navy LT. Commander Edward "Butch" O'Hare, Recipient of the U.S. Congressional Medal of Honor. The busiest U.S. airport is named after him.

The Grumman F4F Wildcat

Much of the USN's air fleet consisted of planes designed and built by Grumman Aircraft Company in Bethpage, Long Island, New York. Leroy Randle "Roy" Grumman (1895-1982) was a genius regarding carrier-based aircraft. Grumman aircraft were built to withstand battle damage. They had added armor shields installed behind the pilot's position for protection and rubberized self-sealing gas tanks. Most importantly, Grumman planes had "fold-back wings." Having aircraft with fold-back wings allowed the USN to stage a greater number of warplanes for carrier takeoffs and landings. As soon as a plane landed, it was lowered via elevator to a lower deck making room for the next plane to land. The first mass-produced folding-wing fighter plane seeing action in WWII was the Grumman F4F Wildcat (below), built at Grumman's factory in Bethpage.

Grumman Corporation diagram
of F4F Wildcat fighter.

Battle of Coral Sea

The first air-sea battle fought at a distance was the Battle of

Coral Sea. In May 1942, the Japanese launched an attack on Port Moresby (Papua-New Guinea). U.S. Naval Intelligence electronically intercepted the Japanese battle plans that enabled the Americans to blunt the attack. After the four-day slugfest ended, the Japanese aircraft carriers *Shoho* and *Shokaku* were sunk. The *USS Saratoga* was sunk, and the USS Yorktown was heavily damaged. The Japanese casualties have been estimated to be from 2,000 to 5,000 killed. The Japanese defeat at Coral Sea not only blunted their aim of invading Port Moresby, the battle loss also prevented the Japanese from gaining control of the South Pacific. There were 543 Americans killed at the Battle of Coral Sea. Though the U.S. Navy made mistakes in tactics early in the war regarding the attack of Japanese carriers and in the defense of their own carriers, the lessons "in blood" learned were neither forgotten nor in vain.

Pacific Ocean battle map and two photographs of ships ablaze at the early WWII Battle of Coral Sea (May 1942).

Along with highly effective USN officer pilots there were also enlisted seamen, many with the rating "Aviation Machinist Mate", who flew in defense of America. In USN slang, these pilots and the sailor aircrews were nicknamed: "Airdales." They were also called "Brown Shoes" after the high top brown shoes they wore while flying. (The sea-going-only sailors wore regulation black shoes.) The enlisted USN Airdales served as air crewmen, airplane repairmen, "spotters" (those that positioned the aircraft on the flight decks), and aircraft chock placers and removers. The Airdales' warplanes were unique and indispensable.

"The propeller and angel wings" insignia
of the U.S. Navy Aviation Machinist Mate.

Grumman's Avenger TBFs / General Motors' Avenger TBMs

After several years of design and testing, Roy Grumman released to the USN on December 7, 1941—by coincidence the same date as the infamous Pearl Harbor attack—the Torpedo-Bomber-Fighter (TBF). As most warplanes were given a word name and a designator of letters and numbers, Roy Grumman named the TBF the "Avenger" in October 1941. The "Avenger" was a most fitting name for the largest single-engine bomber of World War II. Unlike pilot-only F4Fs, Avenger TBFs were substantially larger and had a three-man crew. The crew consisted of: a pilot who could fire a 30-caliber machine gun from the nose of the aircraft; a ball-turret, rear-facing tail gunner, who had a larger 50-caliber machine gun; and a lower level radioman, who was armed with a 30-caliber machine gun called the "Stinger." The Avenger (below) packed a 2,000-pound payload of either bombs or a torpedo in a sturdy fuselage designed to withstand punishment. Large, stable (a handicap in aerial combat), and capable of only relatively slow airspeeds, Avengers were dismissively called "Turkeys." However, the role of these Grumman aircraft and their aircrews was <u>monumental</u> in the Pacific War.

Photographs of Avenger TBFs--one in the air and the other with its engine revving for a "takeoff" from an aircraft carrier.

Heroes of the Battle of Midway and Beyond

On June 4, 1942, Japanese Admiral Isoroku Yamamoto's four aircraft carrier taskforce attacked American-held Midway Island. Six Avenger TBFs from VT-8 squadron flew to Midway Island as a defensive measure. Lieutenant Langdon K. Fieberling was in command of the TBFs. None of the pilots had extensive air combat experience. The six TBFs were launched to repel the huge Japanese fleet attacking Midway Island. They reached the Japanese carriers at 7:10 a.m. and dropped down to horizontal-attack altitude. At that moment, Japanese Mitsubishi Zero warplanes attacked the slow, vulnerable TBFs. Five were immediately shot down with all three-men crews killed. A sixth TBF, piloted by Ensign Albert K. Earnest, dropped his "fish" in the direction of a cruiser. His plane was heavily damaged and barely able to make it back to Midway Island. Earnest's Radioman, 3rd class Harrier H. Ferrier, was wounded. His tail gunner, Seaman 1st class Jay D. Manning, was killed.

Another batch of TBFs, as well as 15, two-crewmen Douglas Company 1934-designed TBD Devastators, were launched from three USN aircraft carriers. Except for one survivor, Ensign Gay, *all* TBF and TBD pilots and crews were KIA (killed in action) without any of their "fish" (torpedoes) hitting enemy ships. At the Battle of Midway, Ensign George Henry Gay (1917-1994), with his tail gunner killed and his plane engulfed in flames, belly-landed his TBD Devastator into the Pacific. Suffering from bullet wounds and burns, Gay languished in the ocean for 30 hours fending off voracious sharks as well as Japanese warplanes strafing him while he placed his "Mae West" life preserver over his head for protection. Ensign Gay was eventually spotted and rescued by a USN PBY Catalina. This incident was depicted in the 1976 movie *Midway*. Gay wrote of his harrowing ordeal in *Sole Survivor of Torpedo Squadron Eight: Battle of Midway* (1980). He retired from the USN as a Lieutenant Commander. Among the many honors Gay received were the Purple Heart, Air Medal, and the U.S. Navy Flying Cross (an award second only to the U.S. Congressional Medal of Honor).

At the Battle of Midway, entire squadrons of Avengers and Devastators were being shot out of the sky. Unlike these USN warplanes that were shot down, a squadron of USN Douglas Dauntless SBD Dive Bombers remained unnoticed by the Japanese aircraft carrier crews. Consequently, Yamamoto's fleet was unprepared to repel the SBDs. In a Dive Bomber attack, the warplane first attains a very high altitude. Then the warplane perilously "plunges" in an almost vertical dive towards a target before releasing a bomb payload. Dive Bomber aircrews often temporarily "black out" while "pulling up" after a diving run. At Midway, the SBDs scored direct hits and sank three Japanese aircraft carriers and a heavy cruiser. The fourth carrier of Yamamoto's taskforce was destroyed shortly thereafter. As each of the Japanese carriers was sunk, Navy pilots proclaimed over crackling aircraft radios: "Scratch one flattop!" The Battle of Midway was a turning point in World War II. Though there would be subsequent massive casualties suffered by the Americans in the Pacific Theater of war, this decisive battle effectively crippled the Japanese armada. On August 24, 1942, twenty-six TBFs from the US aircraft carriers *Saratoga* and *Enterprise* sank the light Japanese aircraft carrier *Ryūjō* off the Eastern Solomon Islands. However, in this attack, seven of the TBFs were shot down. Two months later, TBF crews achieved only modest results damaging Japanese ships at the Battle of Santa Cruz. On the evening of November 13, 1942, USN surface warships severely damaged the huge 37,000-ton Japanese battleship *Hiei* at the naval battle of Guadalcanal. This Japanese battleship escorted Yamamoto's fleet that included aircraft carriers from which Japanese warplanes attacked Pearl Harbor on December 7, 1941. At this November 13 "ship against ship battle," the USN lost two cruisers and four destroyers. On the next morning, USN and USMC Avengers scored direct hits with their "fish" and sank the *Hiei*.

After the attacks on Wake Island and Pearl Harbor, the Americans were on the defensive.

After the Battles of Midway, Eastern Solomons, and Guadalcanal, the Japanese were on the defensive!

An Avenger Pilot who became President and the Father of a President

Massachusetts Senator Prescott Sheldon Bush (1895-1972) was blessed with a son and grandson, who both became president of the United States. During WWII, his son, George Herbert Walker Bush, was an Avenger TBF pilot from the aircraft carrier *USS San Jacinto* (named after the battle where the Texians [spelled with an "i"] were victorious over Mexican dictator Santa Ana's forces following the merciless slaughters at The Alamo and Goliad). G.H.W. Bush was the youngest pilot of WWII having earned his "Navy Wings" three days before his 19th birthday.

Photograph of left-handed LTJG George Herbert Walker Bush writing flight notes in the cockpit of his Avenger TBF.

After more than 50 bombing and strafing missions attacking Japanese ships and fortifications, LTJG Bush's Avenger was hit and heavily damaged by enemy antiaircraft fire from Chi-Chi Jima Island on September 2, 1944 (by coincidence exactly one year before the formal surrender ceremony of the Japanese Empire aboard the battleship *USS Missouri*). With his TBF in flames, Bush banked his aircraft to allow his crewmen to bail out. By this point in time, however, one was already dead. The other crewman, with his parachute aflame, plunged to his death. Bush then bailed out over the Pacific. However, Bush pulled his "ripcord" prematurely. In doing so, the tail wing of his TBF struck his forehead. Though stunned and bleeding profusely, Bush made it safely to the sea though he was certainly not out of danger. Dazed from a head injury and treading water to stay afloat, he could not locate his life raft. Fellow TBF pilots circling overhead spotted Bush's floatation device. Through hand signals, they pointed to where Bush needed to swim to grasp his life raft. However, Bush's life raft was caught in a strong current headed *back* towards Chi-Chi Jima Island. In addition, a Japanese patrol boat was on its way to capture Bush. TBF pilots circling overhead strafed the Japanese vessel, which was then forced to return to shore. After four tense hours on a leaky life raft just a few miles off the coast of the Chi-Chi Jima Island, the submarine, USS Finback, rescued the twenty-year old Avenger pilot. (70 Years Ago Yesterday#1B89F47; Retrieved 2/29/2016). LTJG Bush fortunately did not parachute *over* Chi-Chi Jima Island. Had he landed on the Japanese-held archipelago, he would have most likely been caught and beheaded. This was a grisly fate that befell eight of his fellow pilots and crewmen, who had previously parachuted or crash-landed on the island. In fact, the Japanese commander of Chi-Chi Jima Island was later charged with war crimes. Among his misdeeds was the literal butchering of captured U.S. Navy airmen. The Japanese commander roasted the livers and thighs of executed USN airmen for dinner. After the war, the Japanese military commander was brought to justice. After a lengthy trial, he was found guilty and hung for his crimes. (George Bush's comrades #1B89F48; Retrieved 2/29/2106).

The Bravery of the U.S. Navy "Airdales"

By the time of their 50th combat mission, USN pilots were nearing battle fatigue due to the many hazards they faced on each mission. These pilots had to "takeoff" and land on windswept, wave-pitching aircraft carriers. When landing, their aircraft "tail hooks" had to catch one of the carriers "arresting wires." Pilots who approached the carrier at an angle or at speeds that were too fast or slow were given the "Wave Off" by landing officers, who often were pilots themselves. Disregarding the "Wave off" resulting in a pilot being "grounded" for disobeying USN regulations. Aircraft that landed but missed the "arresting wires" were unable to stop. These planes and crews outran the flight deck and went overboard into the "brink." [The author's father sat, as a rear-facing gunner, on Avengers during the war. When his TBF landed on the carrier and was stopped by the "arresting wire," the author's father thanked God by "making the sign of the cross."]

During the Pacific War, USN pilots and crewmen faced an additional difficulty. Frequently, there was "radio silence"--a tense period when radio contact between planes and carriers was prohibited to prevent the Japanese from pinpointing the location of the American flattops. Unable to contact and find their carriers, pilots flew their planes in a desperate search until fuel ran out. If this happened, they crashed into the ocean—often, never to be seen again. Even if the naval flyers survived landings at sea, they then often spent countless hours on life rafts with only a lucky few being rescued. On carrier flight decks, many sailors were injured or killed while walking carelessly into aircraft propellers. The "Airdales" were taught to "walk directly forward or 90 degrees to the left or right"—never diagonally where they were more likely to be "cut in half" by spinning propeller blades. In Edward Atkins' (2006) *Flight Deck: A Day in the Life of an Airdale*, the author, a retired USN Petty Officer, characterizes his book as: "...a tribute to all the Airdales, they who served unstintingly, often under extremely difficult, arduous, harrowing conditions, EACH day, for months on end" (p. xv). Atkins poses the eternal question: "Where do you find such men?" The response is the nation has *always* found such men—and women--in all of its wars. Stated another way: Their valor helps define American exceptionalism!

U.S. Navy Airdale Burial At Sea; GM builds TBMs

On November 5, 1944, Avenger TBFs from the carrier *USS Essex* launched an attack at the Battle of Manila Bay in the Philippines. During the attack, the tail gunner of Avenger #93, USN Aviation Machinist Mate 2nd Class Loyce Edward Deen, was instantaneously killed in his tail gunner position by a blast of 40 millimeter Japanese anti-aircraft shellfire. The heavily damaged TBF, expertly piloted by Lt. Robert Cosgrove, barely made it back to *The Essex*. Spare airplane parts while at sea were scarce. However, U.S. Navy authorities ordered that Deen's Avenger not be scavenged. Petty Officer Deen was buried at sea within his TBF. This poignant event concludes the documentary *Victory at Sea* episode entitled: "The Conquest of Micronesia." A more complete video of Deen's sea burial is available at: (www.criticalpast.com/video/65675070253_tbf-avenger-aircraft_uss-essex_sea-burial_dead-gunner; Retrieved 2/29/2016.)

Due to the rapid attrition of warplanes in the Pacific War, the U.S. Navy was requisitioning an ever-growing number of Avengers. In coordination with the U.S. War Department, the task of building Avengers was transferred from Grumman to the much larger facilities of General Motors. By late 1943, Avengers were made solely at GM manufacturing plants in North Tarrytown, Westchester County, NY, as well as other GM factories across the country. Avengers built by GM were designated TBMs. Grumman's Long Island facilities were then used to manufacture F6F Hellcats.

The Grumman F6F Hellcat

Grumman's F6F Hellcats had engines with superchargers that delivered twice the horsepower of F4F Wildcat engines. Not only were Hellcats far superior to Wildcats, they were also far more capable than their Japanese archrival, the Mitsubishi A6M Zero. U.S. Navy and Marine aviators flying Hellcats attained a superb war record. Hellcats contained six 50-caliber wing-mounted Browning machine guns that ripped apart less armored Japanese warplanes. The Japanese Zero may have been a little more maneuverable, but the F6Fs were faster and packed a more lethal array of machine guns. All told, F6F pilots achieved a stellar 19 to 1 kill ratio and were responsible for over 75 percent of all aerial victories by American aircraft in the Pacific War (http://militaryhistory.about.com/od/worldwariiaircraft/p/f6f-hellcat.htm; Retrieved 2/29/2016.)

Indiana-born Alex Vraciu (1918-2015) was the proverbial "Ace of Aces." Piloting Hellcats, Vraciu shot down 19 Japanese planes and destroyed another 21 that were on the ground. Vraciu scored his victories during the pivotal Pacific battle known as the "Great Marianas Turkey Shoot" in the Philippine Sea that spanned two days, June 19-20, 1944. Awarded the U.S. Navy Cross, Vraciu was given the nickname: "Grumman's Best Customer." In 2010, the Indiana Historical Society published a biography of Vraciu written by Ray E. Boomhower entitled: *Fighter Pilot: The WWII Career of Alex Vraciu.* Passing away on January 29, 2015, Vraciu was up to that time the nation's highest scoring *living WWII "Ace."*

Two photographs of Grumman F6F Hellcat fighters.

U.S. Navy "Airdales" Honored in Film and Music

Recognizing the vital role of USN flyers, Hollywood produced a slew of movies that included aerial combat film footage taken from gun cameras mounted on Grumman and other warplanes. The film: *A Wing and a Prayer: The Story of Carrier X* accurately portrays the sacrifice and ultimate triumph of the USN flyers. In the film, the viewer sees a blackboard listing TBF squadron members. By the film's end, most of the names listed on the blackboard had been erased. These erased names were USN pilots killed in action. Prolific movie score composer Max Steiner and lyricist Gus Kahn co-wrote a theme that was used in many WWII-era films, especially those depicting the U.S. Navy. Steiner's music and Kahn's words honor those American sailors who fought in the air. The Steiner/Kahn theme is: "We Watch the Skyways!"

We watch the skyways;
O'er the land and the sea;
Ready to fly anywhere the duty calls;
Ready to fight to be free!"

The following is a sample of four films that used this Steiner/Kahn composition: *Dive Bomber*, *Fighter Squadron*, *Operation Pacific*, and *Up Periscope*.

The Fighting Lady: The Lady and the Sea

Perhaps the most complete WWII film depicting aircraft carriers and their crews was a documentary called: *The Fighting Lady: The Lady and the Sea* (1945). This film was directed by William Wyler and narrated by actor Robert Taylor--both at the time USN officers. The movie depicts life on an *unnamed* aircraft carrier amidst the Pacific War. After WWII, the name of the carrier was revealed. It was the *USS Yorktown*. One can only imagine the adrenaline rush and sheer anxiousness of air crews upon hearing the order "piping" over the carrier's public address system: *"Pilots, Man Your Planes!"* The film focuses on a number of aviators, especially one nicknamed "Smokey." The documentary ends with a montage of pilots killed in action--including "Smokey."

U.S. Navy pilots discussing an impending mission aboard one of America's "flattops."

The Enlisted Airdales Get Their "A C Wings"

In 1958, the U.S. Department of Defense began awarding "U.S. Navy Air Crewman Wings" to *enlisted* sailors who flew in combat missions.

Above is a 1960s photograph of a flight crew in front of a propeller-driven U.S. Navy plane about to takeoff in performing anti-submarine duties along the Atlantic coastline of the U.S.A. At the extreme right of the photo is the author's father, Chief Petty Officer Daniel C. Marrone. For his combat service in USN warplanes, D. C. Marrone was awarded the U.S. Navy "Air Crewman Wings." He passed away on April 24, 1999. Prominently etched on the granite gravestone below his name is inscribed:

U.S. Navy E-9 ★★.

Below are the "A C Wings" and the 1942-1943 U.S. Navy Roundel insignia that appeared on the fuselage and wings of Grumman- manufactured Wildcats, Avengers, and (early-produced) Hellcats during the first two years of World War II.

United States Navy Air Crewman "A C Wings."

United States Navy Roundel insignia painted
on Grumman warplanes (1942-1943).

Chapter 7
Brigadier General Hugh Mercer: "Jacobite" Rebel and Hero of the American Revolutionary War

The life of Dr. Hugh Mercer could easily be viewed as "fiction" given the many episodes in which he faced peril. Mercer was a refugee from Scotland following the failed Jacobite (follower of James II) Rebellion to overthrow the regime of British King George II. The rebellion can be traced to the "Restoration" of King Charles II in England on May 25, 1660. On this day, Charles II regained the throne of the kingdoms of England, Scotland, and Ireland. On his deathbed in February 1685, Charles II was given "Last Rites" by a Roman Catholic priest. He was succeeded by his younger brother James, Duke of York, who became King James II. Unlike his brother, King James II was not reticent about declaring his religious faith. He was overtly Roman Catholic.

Paintings of King James II, King William III, and Queen Mary II.

The ascension of Catholic King James II to the English throne in 1685 created a crisis for the Protestant majority-led English Parliament. The Protestants feared a return to Catholicism in their nation's monarchy. When James II bore a son that was baptized as a Roman Catholic, the English Parliament deposed James II. This pivotal event was called the "Glorious Revolution" and the "Revolution of 1688." Parliamentary leaders then offered the English throne to the Protestant Dutch *stadtholder* William of Orange, who was wed to James II's Protestant daughter: Mary Stuart. William of Orange demanded that he be made king and his wife made queen. Thus, for the first and only time during the past millennium, England had co-regents: "William and Mary." Queen Mary II died in 1694. Fearing that the death of William would provide an opportunity for a Roman Catholic to ascend to the throne, Parliament passed the Act of Settlement in 1701 that contained a provision barring Catholics from attaining the crown of England. Less than a year later, William III died and Anne Stuart, a Protestant, assumed the throne as "Queen Anne." Her coronation was held on March 8, 1702.

The Parliament of England and the Parliament of Scotland both had a majority of Protestant members who were in favor of permitting only Protestants as monarchs. Also, a majority in both legislatures were in favor of combining the monarchy into one nation, Great Britain. The Treaty of Union (July 22, 1706) brought together England, Wales, and Scotland into one nation and also contained a permanent prohibition of Catholics ascending to the now, combined throne. As of May 1, 1707, their legislatures were also combined. As of that date, there was one legislative body: the Parliament of Great Britain. When Queen Anne died in 1714, her closest Protestant relative was not to be found in Great Britain but rather in the German principality of Hanover. George, the Elector of Hanover, ascended to the British throne as King George I (1660-1727). His son, George Augustus of Hanover, became British King George II (1683-1760). Officially, these Hanovers were British monarchs. However, this did not satisfy quite a few Britons, who stubbornly refused to accept the German-speaking Hanover princes as their monarchs. As a consequence, there were numerous rebel uprisings. The most pivotal of these insurrections occurred in Scotland.

Paintings of "Bonnie Prince Charlie" in his youth.

The Jacobite Rebellion

Deposed James II's grandson, Charles Edward Louis John Casimir Sylvester Severino Maria Stuart (1720-1788), was derisively called the "Young Pretender" to the British throne. Born in Rome of Italian, Polish, Portuguese, and Scottish ancestry, "Bonnie Prince Charlie" led the failed Jacobite (followers of James II) Rebellion. These Jacobite rebels were adamantly in favor of deposing the Hanovers and restoring the Stuarts to the British throne. At first, the rebels were victorious, particularly at the Battle of Prestonpans on September 21, 1745, against larger but disorganized Hanoverian armies. Other small Jacobite victories followed until Prince William Augustus, the fearsomely effective Duke of Cumberland (1721-1765), was appointed commander of the Hanoverian army. With Lord Cumberland as "Captain-General," the rebels were now "outgeneraled" as well as being outnumbered. It was only a matter of time before the Jacobite uprising would collapse. This occurred at the climactic Battle of Culloden on April 16, 1746. Lord Cumberland was merciless in rooting out and slaughtering rebels. For his lack of mercy, he has been called "Butcher Cumberland." The leader of the defeated rebels, "Bonnie Prince Charlie," hid for several weeks among the Highlanders (*Hieland men*) loyal to his Jacobite cause. Through the assistance of Flora MacDonald, he escaped capture and sailed away from the British Isles--never to return. The Scots of yesteryear and of today lament the loss of their hero in a poem composed by Carolina Oliphant (Lady Nairne; 1766-1845): "Will Ye No Come Back Again?" also titled "Bonnie Charlie." This poem was set to an old Scottish folk tune and has been described by Caroline Hazard in 1901 as follows: "Who that hears 'Bonnie Charlie' sung is touched by that longing for the unattainable which is the blessing and the despair of the idealist?"

"Bonnie Prince Charlie," leader of the Jacobite Rebellion wearing the Scotland-colored "Blue Bonnet."

Scottish followers of deposed King James II called "Jacobites." (*Jacob* is the Hebrew name for James.)

Mercer's Early Life

As personal physician to "Bonnie Prince Charlie," Dr. Hugh Mercer was exceedingly high on Lord Cumberland's "most wanted" list of Jacobite rebels to be caught. Mercer was born on January 17, 1726 to William Mercer and Ann Monro Mercer. His father was a Presbyterian minister at the Pitsligo Parish Church. Extremely bright, young Hugh quickly mastered his studies and was admitted, at age 15, to the Marischal College of Medicine, a component of the prestigious University of Aberdeen. He graduated in 1744, at the tender age of 18, as a qualified doctor and surgeon. A year later, he joined the Jacobite uprising as physician to "Bonnie Prince Charlie." When the Jacobite rebellion failed, Mercer evaded capture and certain execution by fleeing incognito to colonial America. His ship landed in Philadelphia in May 1747. To further avoid being captured by the British, Mercer ventured to the sparsely populated western portion of the Pennsylvania Colony. The Scot refugee practiced medicine in a rustic setting so remote that he was the sole fully trained physician. This frontier outpost would later be named Mercersburg. After seven years of relative tranquility, Mercer was again fighting. This time as a militia captain and physician tending the survivors of British Major General Edward Braddock's disastrous campaign against the French-held Fort Duquesne located in today's Pittsburgh. In an ironic twist, the fugitive Jacobite rebel that was *sought for treason by the British* joined the Pennsylvania Provisional militia fighting *along side the British* during the French and Indian War (1754-1763). This New World conflict spread to Europe and the Asian subcontinent two years later and became known as the "Seven Years' War" (1756-1763). In late summer 1756, Ireland-born British Lieutenant Colonel John Armstrong (1717-1795) led a successful, joint British Redcoat and Pennsylvania militia attack on Native American Delaware and Shawnee warriors, who were attacking settlements west of the Allegheny Mountains. On September 8, 1756, Armstrong's men destroyed *Kit-Han-Ne* (Kittanning) village. As a result, the defeated Delaware and Shawnee warriors ceased their raids on these settlements.

Kittanning village historic marker in Pennsylvania.

Hugh Mercer was severely wounded in the right arm at the Battle of Kittanning. Unconscious and with serious injuries, he was presumed to have died and thus was abandoned on the battlefield. Remarkably, he regained consciousness. Seriously wounded and alone, Mercer trod on foot over 100 miles to Fort Shirley. With unbridled stamina and sheer determination, the stalwart militia captain managed to survive serious injuries, starvation, predatory animals, and vengeful Indian warriors to eventually reach safety and recuperate from his 14-day ordeal. Mercer returned to Philadelphia as a hero and was awarded the "Silver Medal" by the City of Brotherly Love. He served four additional years in the militia and left military service with the rank of full colonel. After nine years of brutal fighting, the French and Indian War ended with the Treaty of Paris that was signed on February 10, 1763.

Dr. Hugh Mercer in Virginia; The American Revolution Commences

At the suggestion of Virginia Militia Colonel George Washington, Mercer moved to the Old Dominion city of Fredericksburg in 1760. Running through this burgeoning trading post is the Rappahannock River. (In Algonquin language, it means "river of quick, rising water where the tide ebbs and flows.") Here he established a medical practice with a physician's apothecary. Among his growing list of patients was Mary Ball Washington (1708-1789), the mother of the "Father of the Country." This northern Virginia village also included a sizable number of Scots who had recently immigrated to colonial America. One of these families, named Gordon, owned a popular tavern in the heart of Fredericksburg. Mercer married the tavern owner's daughter, Isabella Gordon. They had five children: Ann Mercer, who married Robert Patton and from which the notable WWII general is surnamed; John Mercer; William Mercer; George Weedon Mercer; and Hugh Tennant Mercer.

The French and Indian War was a global conflict that drained Great Britain's financial resources. Seeking to recoup these expenditures, the British Parliament enacted a series of ill-conceived, inequitably implemented, and extremely unpopular confiscatory taxes to be paid by American colonists. Acerbating the growing rift with Great Britain was the colonists' view that they were denied representation in the British Parliament, which was levying these "coercive and intolerable" tax acts. After numerous incidents, such as the Boston Massacre (1770) and the Boston Tea Party (1773), British authorities and the American colonists were at the brink of war. The actual first shot of the war occurred on April 19, 1775, when the British Redcoats and the Minutemen of Massachusetts clashed at Lexington and Concord.

Hugh Mercer was appointed to the Committee of Safety in Fredericksburg that year. However, he was at first denied the leadership of the Virginia regiment due to his "northern British birth." Resourceful and determined, Mercer formed the "Minute Men of Spotsylvania, King George, Stafford, and Caroline Counties" in November 1775. With his obvious acumen for leadership, Mercer readily overcame any hesitation from the Committee of Safety, which commissioned him Colonel of the 3rd Virginia Regiment on January 11, 1776. Under his command were many future American leaders, including U.S. Supreme Court Chief Justice John Marshall and the fifth U.S. president James Monroe. The American Continental Congress commissioned Mercer a "Brigadier General" in June 1776. His first task was to construct Fort Lee. Named for British-born American Major General Charles Lee (1732-1782), the fort was sited along the New Jersey Palisades overlooking the Hudson River. On November 16, 1776, British Regulars combined with Hessian mercenaries swiftly conquered the last American Patriot bastion on Manhattan Island: Fort Washington. All 2,800 Continental Army soldiers in the fort were either killed or became prisoners of war rotting away in dreadful British ships anchored in New-York Harbor. On the opposite side of the Hudson River from Fort Washington was Fort Lee, which was abandoned by the Americans four days later. With no Patriot strongholds impeding the British/Hessian juggernaut, many areas of New York and New Jersey fell under the control of the Crown forces led by British Major General William Howe.

Battles of Trenton and Princeton

In December 1776, Mercer's Virginia regiment crossed the Delaware River into Pennsylvania awaiting orders from General Washington. By this time, the Continental Army was perhaps at its lowest ebb with barely 3,000 effectives—those fit to fight. Adding to this distress was the fact that many of the army enlistments were due to expire on December 31, 1776. The "American Cause for Independence" was collapsing. In a last ditch attempt to keep the Continental Army intact, the Commander-in-Chief devised a plan to cross the partially frozen Delaware River into New Jersey and attack a Hessian garrison in Trenton. Though Mercer fully supported Washington's plan, many other high-ranking officers were opposed, fearing little or no possibility for success. Nevertheless, the plan was implemented on Christmas Day, December 25, 1776. Washington ordered Dunham cargo boats launched from McKonkey's Ferry to bring the bedraggled Continental Army across the icy Delaware River. As the weather worsened, crossing the river became impossible. Therefore, a major contingent of Continental soldiers never made it across the Delaware due to the severe weather. The last of the Americans that did reach New Jersey arrived on the morning of December 26, which delayed General Washington's battle plan.

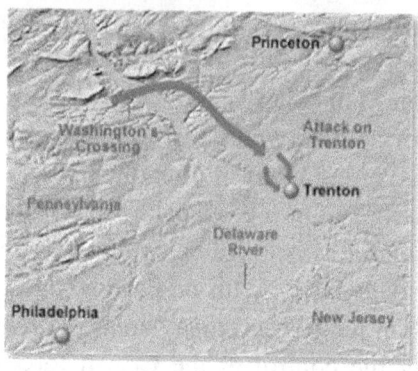

Map of General Washington crossing the
Delaware River to the Battle of Trenton on December 26, 1776.

The Hessians at Trenton were under the command of Colonel Johann Rahl (1726-1776), who was dismissive of the Continental Army's ability and willingness to fight. The Americans refuted Rahl's assessment by boldly attacking and utterly defeating the Hessian battalion while sustaining only two casualties: George Washington's cousin, Artillery Captain William Washington (1752-1810) and Lieutenant James Monroe (1758-1831). As well as scoring a much-needed military triumph, the victory at Trenton spurred new enlistments in the nearly depleted Continental Army. During the following days, the Americans crossed back and forth between Pennsylvania and New Jersey. General Washington was eager to follow up the victory at Trenton. On January 2, 1777, Washington ordered his men to attack what was assumed to be the rear guard of Howe's army at Princeton, a village 13 miles north of Trenton. The Americans were misinformed because what they encountered were "crack troops" under the command of the formidable British Major General Charles Lord Cornwallis.

Compared to the June 1778 Battle of Monmouth Courthouse, the January 2-3, 1777 Battle of Princeton involved fewer combatants.

However, the Princeton battle was nevertheless a significant victory for the Americans. On the second day of battle, the 1,200-man Continental Army brigade, under the command of Brigadier General Mercer, fought a heavily experienced 800-Redcoat contingent of Cornwallis' army, under the command of Lieutenant Colonel Charles Mawhood. In the melee, Mercer's horse was shot; and now the fiery Scottish-American was skirmishing on foot. The Redcoats surrounded Mercer, who they may have mistook for General Washington. Ordered to surrender, Mercer instead drew his sword and slashed at the British Regulars. Surrounded, Mercer was beat over the head with rifle butts and stabbed seven times with bayonets. With their commander severely wounded, Mercer's troops began retreating. General Washington stemmed this retreat by personally leading a frontal charge attacking the British. Through the sacrificial bravery of Mercer, and with Washington's valor under fire, the tide of battle reversed with the Redcoats now fleeing the Princeton battlefield.

"The Death of General Mercer at the Battle of Princeton"
by John Trumbull (1756-1843).

Brigadier General Mercer was grievously wounded in this battle, which ended on January 3, 1777. He was brought to the Thomas Clarke House for medical treatment and was attended by the illustrious American physician: Dr. Benjamin Rush (1746-1813). As an experienced doctor who tended to many wounded soldiers,

Mercer knew that his own wounds were fatal. In a final stubborn fight to survive, Hugh Mercer lasted nine days before dying on January 12, 1777. His body was brought to the Christ Church Burial Ground in Philadelphia for internment with full military honors. Mercer was widely acclaimed an American hero. His name graces many American cities, counties, townships, forts, and streets. His legacy does not end there. His five children and their descendants would become an array of famous statesmen and generals that fought in all of America's wars. One of these was "Blood and Guts" four-star U.S. Army General George Smith Patton, Jr. (1885-1945), who was a leader of the U.S. Army in defeating the Nazis in World War II. His son, Major General George Smith Patton III (1923-2004), was a heroic leader of the U.S. Army in the Korean and Vietnam Wars. For his bravery under fire, G. S. Patton III was awarded two Distinguished Service Crosses as well as the Purple Heart. Another descendent was the prolific singer, songwriter, lyricist, and record company executive John Herndon "Johnny" Mercer (1909-1976). The United States is exceedingly fortunate to have had Scottish physician Hugh Mercer emigrate to the U.S.A. He and his illustrious family attained greatness for their nation.

Portrait of Continental Army Brigadier General Hugh Mercer.

A direct descendant of Continental Army Brigadier General Hugh Mercer was WWII four-star General George Smith Patton, Jr. His statue proudly stands at the U.S. Military Academy at West Point. The next photograph is of singer/songwriter John Herndon "Johnny" Mercer at the piano.
(Public domain photographs.)

References

Hazard, C. (1901). The Value of History in the Formation of Character. *The School Review, 9,* p. 10.

Waterman, J. M. (1941). *With Sword and Lancet: The Life of General Hugh Mercer.* Richmond, VA: Garrett and Massie.

Chapter 8
Martha Washington Visits General George Washington at the Continental Army Encampments

Pulitzer Prize-winning biographer James Thomas Flexner (1908-2003) referred to George Washington as the "Indispensable Man." While Flexner was eminently correct in his tribute, Martha Washington's care and comfort to her husband was substantial and enduring. With Martha's nurture, General Washington was able to lead his men for eight arduous years throughout the American Revolutionary War (1775-1783), with only a few days leave of absence. Martha helped the general emotionally and physically to withstand the huge stresses brought upon by disastrous battlefield losses as well as the deaths of beloved friends such as Brigadier General Hugh Mercer. Although the iconic George Washington is invariably depicted as a towering figure--both in terms of physical height and prestige--the Virginian's health, although in the main robust, was at times very poor. During the war and the 16 years that followed, George suffered from the following maladies: croup, quinsy, Ludwig's angina, Vincent's angina, diphtheria, streptococcal throat infections, and acute bacterial epiglottitis—any one of which could have been fatal. Debate has continued concerning which of these maladies did indeed cause his death on December 14, 1799. Except for a few days visit to his Mount Vernon home in Virginia just prior to the September/October 1781 Battle of Yorktown, General Washington led his troops throughout the war in battles occurring in Connecticut, Delaware, Maryland, Massachusetts, New Jersey,

New York, Pennsylvania, Rhode Island, and Virginia.

Typical northeast winter weather included mountainous snow and ice storms that made primitive roads nearly impassible. Yet, Martha left her comfortable Mount Vernon home to be with her husband nearly every winter. At these frozen encampments, many Continental soldiers died from disease, malnutrition, and, of course, bitterly cold weather. The Valley Forge encampment, from December 19, 1777 through June 19, 1778, was especially harsh with prolonged periods of icy weather and inadequate food and supplies. One-quarter of the Continental Army perished due to disease and freezing temperatures. Martha's presence at Valley Forge helped her husband overcome daunting living conditions. There was also a new arrival at Valley Forge from Europe named Baron von Steuben. The former Prussian military officer helped significantly by disciplining and training American militiamen into an effective fighting force.

Three years later, the Americans, with the monumental help of the French army and navy, achieved a decisive victory at Yorktown on the Virginia peninsular. Following the 1781 victory at Yorktown, there were two more years of tenseness and uncertainty between the British and the Americans while a peace treaty was being negotiated in Paris. Though only small skirmishes occurred during these two years, intense restiveness among the troops persisted. These tensions affected the morale throughout the Continental Army. Officers and soldiers were unpaid and denied permission to leave for home.

Martha Washington—Early Life

Martha "Patsy" Dandridge was born on June 2, 1731, and was the oldest child of a large brood of three brothers and five sisters. Martha's parents, John Dandridge and Frances Jones, owned sizable farming acreage in Chestnut Grove within the southeastern region of the Virginia Colony. In 1750, at the age of 18, she married Daniel Parke Custis, born in 1711, who came from a wealthy plantation owning family. With Parke Custis, Martha bore four children—all having the middle name "Parke" as an inheritance requirement. Two of their children, Daniel Parke Custis II (1751–1754) and Frances Parke Custis (1753–1757), died in childhood. On July 8, 1757, Martha's husband passed away, leaving her with a vast estate of lucrative tobacco plantations comprising more than 17,779 acres. With the death of her husband, Martha was left a widow—an exceedingly rich one. Along with being a trustee of the inheritances of her two remaining children, Jacky and Patsy, Martha also had her own independent dower inheritance of 23,000 pounds sterling as well as bank stock in England. Her wealth combined with her attractive features made Martha the focus of many suitors, including Charles Carter, 24 years her senior and a scion of the Old Dominion Lancaster County clan of Robert "King" Carter, one of the wealthiest men in the American Colonies.

However tempting Charles Carter's overtures, it was a 6-foot, 3-inch, 26-year-old Virginia Militia colonel named George Washington, eight months her junior, who attracted her attention. George visited Martha several times during the early part of 1758. On June 5, they announced their engagement. Eagerly seeking prominence in Virginia society, George Washington ran for and was elected one month later to the House of Burgesses representing Frederick County. He would go on to serve 16 years in the House of Burgesses. In December 1758, the future Continental Army Commander-in-Chief resigned his militia commission. Now out of military service, Washington wore civilian attire at his wedding to Martha on January 6, 1759.

Computer generated image of Martha Washington created by anthropologists using a 1796 portrait to show how she may have looked at age 28 when she married George Washington. (Courtesy of illustrator Michael J. Deas, *The Washington Post*).

George Washington ably fulfilled the role of country squire overseeing the home and lands he inherited from his half brother, Lawrence. Upon marriage to Martha, he also controlled vast plantations generating sizable income. In addition, he had to manage Martha's dowries and the financial trusts of her two surviving children, Patsy and Jacky Parke Custis. George cherished Martha's children. Unfortunately, both died at a young age. Martha ("Patsy") Parke Custis, born in 1756, suffered from epilepsy. George was devastated when Patsy suffered a fatal seizure on June 19, 1773. John ("Jacky") Parke Custis, born in 1754, died before reaching age 27. Against his mother's stern admonitions, Jacky joined his stepfather as a military aide at the siege of Yorktown. While there, Jacky contracted typhoid fever and died on November 5, 1781. In an age when medical treatment was nonexistent or at best crude, the always-nurturing Martha had to cope with the frequent illnesses and deaths of many members of her large extended family. Amid a constant flurry of houseguests and the administration of vast plantations, she and George remained loving and content. Turbulent events in their country, however, forced the couple to soon face extreme hardships.

The War for Independence

Following the French and Indian War, the relationship between Great Britain and her thirteen American colonies was becoming increasingly strained and untenable. On June 1, 1774, George Washington, still a member of the Virginia House of Burgesses, participated in a day of fasting and prayer in solidarity with the beleaguered Massachusetts Colony. The British ordered Boston Harbor closed as a punishment for the vandalism caused by the "Sons of Liberty." This act of sabotage on British property was the original "Tea Party." (In today's lexicon, "Tea Party" refers to individuals, consisting for the most part of conservative political activists, who are unhappy with high-tax liberal social and economic policies.) For this 1774 act of vandalism, the British ended the right of Bostonians to convene a legislative body. Responding to this British heavy-handedness, the American colonies each sent representatives to a newly formed Continental Congress in Philadelphia. On September 5, 1774, the American legislators began discussing economic and political problems ranging from illegal British taxation to the eventual complete independence from the British. George Washington was chosen to represent Virginia at the Continental Congress. On June 15, 1775, at the Second Continental Congress, Massachusetts representative John Adams nominated George Washington to be the general and Commander-in-Chief of the Continental Army. The Virginian accepted this monumental task. Arriving in Boston, General Washington faced the disorderliness and filth generated by hundreds of untrained militiamen reluctant to observe commonsense cleanliness. The militiamen also sometimes refused to obey the orders of officers. All this resulted in poor, unacceptable military discipline. General Washington quickly ordered measures to instill discipline and enacted various levels of punishment on those who did not follow orders.

Washington was always properly clad in military uniform and sword. His demeanor never caused ambiguity. He was in command! This did not mean that Washington was an unfeeling martinet. He stoically bore the stress of commanding a ragtag, untrained army in the making. With these burdens, Washington requested that his wife immediately join him in Boston. On November 16, 1775, Martha began the first of many trips to army encampments to be with her husband. Venturing from the comfort of her sumptuous Mount Vernon home, Martha rode carriages on crude, bumpy roads to be with her husband. Since substantial bridges did not exist during her era, she was also forced to cross seemingly countless rivers on open ferryboats. Her first journey took an arduous 25 days. Martha's unwavering motivation, then and throughout the war, was to comfort her husband. After she set the pattern of journeying to army encampments, many wives of Continental Army officers and soldiers followed Martha's example. The visits of wives to the encampments diminished the boredom and health problems prevalent during long northeast winters, when armies were unequipped for battle in frigid weather. Martha stayed at Cambridge over the typically harsh Boston winter until April 4, 1776. She then traveled south. However, she did not go directly to Mount Vernon. Instead, she stayed briefly in New-York City awaiting her husband. Once together, they traveled next to Philadelphia. Arriving on May 23, Martha was inoculated for smallpox—an essential though highly risky treatment during this era. After overcoming the side effects of the smallpox vaccine, she began traveling back and forth between New-York City and Philadelphia during the summer of 1776. Mindful of Martha's safety in precariously vulnerable Manhattan Island, Washington requested that she stay in Philadelphia throughout August. Shortly thereafter, she rode back to Mount Vernon where she was kept fully occupied in running their vast estate. A delightful array of grandnieces and grandnephews kept her very busy.

Aside from the momentous signing of the Declaration of Independence on July 4, 1776, events were beginning to look ominous for the Americans as the British and Hessian troops were massing hundreds of warships crowded in New-York Bay preparing to launch an invasion that became the Battles of Long Island and New-York. These engagements combined with the Battle of White Plains were all disastrous defeats for the Americans. The Continental Army scored small but quite significant victories at Trenton in December 1776 and at Princeton in January 1777. In the first months of 1777, the Americans were ensconced at their Morristown encampment in the northern part of New Jersey. To call Morristown an "encampment" is an overstatement, because no shelters were erected for the soldiers. Instead, the Continentals stayed with local families and faced what would be a repeated pattern of coping with inadequate levels of shelter, food, ammunition, and supplies. In February, word reached Martha that George was suffering from a severe sore throat, referred to at the time as "quinsy." (The present term for this illness is "peritonsillar abscess." Washington would periodically suffer from this malady, and it may have been the cause of his death on December 14, 1799.) As soon as Martha heard of his illness, she left Mount Vernon for Morristown. After spending nearly a month traveling on primitive, gutted roads, further hindered by blizzard conditions, she finally reached her husband in New Jersey. Martha brought with her wagonloads of food, medicine, and cloth--the latter of which was made from flax grown at Mount Vernon. She also brought intangible assistance—as she would throughout the war. This was her "let's-get-to-work" mindset. Thus, Martha was remarkable for her ability to effectively cope with disheartening circumstances. At Morristown, she began to set up social events to help boost morale. Martha conducted sewing circles and hosted simple-fare dinner parties for the officers and their wives. With her husband back in good health, she left New Jersey in June 1777. Martha's next immediate concern was her pregnant daughter in-law, Eleanor ("Nelly") Calvert Custis. Nelly married John Parke Custis when he was 18 and she was 16. On the last day of 1777, Nelly gave birth to her second daughter, Martha ("Patsy") Parke Custis, at Mount Vernon.

Martha Washington at Valley Forge

Needed by her rapidly growing family at Mount Vernon, Martha nevertheless was again "called to duty" to Pennsylvania by her husband in January 1778. A month earlier, the Continental Army camped at Valley Forge. This was a desolate flat plain of land that was easily defendable against the British, who were occupying nearby Philadelphia. Situated along the Schuylkill River in southeastern Pennsylvania, Washington called this Valley Forge encampment "a dreary kind of place." Undernourished soldiers performed sentry duty without shoes for protection against frozen ground. Martha arrived at the encampment after nearly a month of travel, bearing wagonloads of supplies for her husband's desperate soldiers. Prior to Martha's arrival, General Washington, in solidarity with his men, was living in a tent. Once Martha arrived, he and his wife lodged at the small Isaacs Potts house, located at the confluence of Valley Creek with the Schuylkill River. This temporary home would also serve as the general's headquarters. Soon after her arrival, Martha started to organize group activities. She formed sewing circles to darn shirts and socks and made daily visits to the hordes of sick soldiers suffering from typhus, typhoid, dysentery, and pneumonia. During the encampment an estimated 2,500 out of the 10,000 to 12,000 soldiers billeted at Valley Forge died from disease. For entertainment—and no doubt to get everyone's mind off of the dreadful circumstances—Martha organized singing groups to bring warmth and hope to the camp. The arrival of a new officer helped to transform the Americans from a loose combination of state militias into a cohesive fighting force.

This was former Prussian Army Lieutenant General Baron Friedrich Wilhelm August Heinrich von Steuben. The non-English speaking officer came to the Pennsylvania encampment bearing a complimentary letter of recommendation from American Ambassador to France, Benjamin Franklin. In truth, Baron von Steuben was only a captain in the Prussian army. Furthermore, he was discharged from the army due to undisclosed reasons. And he was not a Baron. Thus, the "von" in his name was most likely fictitious. Nonetheless, Baron von Steuben's role at Valley Forge was pivotal for he expertly and tirelessly trained the disorganized militiamen into a formidable fighting force. The Baron also wrote the first field-training manual for the Continental Army that is still an official document of the United States Army. On February 6, 1778, French King Louis XVI signed the "Treaty of Alliance" bonding France with the newly recognized United States of America. Along with the welcome announcement of the signing of the treaty with France, springtime weather finally came to frozen Valley Forge. The rising temperatures thawed icy roads, thus allowing more food to be brought into Valley Forge. These two factors boosted morale. General Washington ordered a massive parade in honor of the new grand alliance in May 1778. As the Continentals passed in review in front of General and Lady Washington, the soldiers displayed the camaraderie, pride, and swagger of a "winning army." Martha left her husband to return to Virginia on June 9. Overcoming the hardships and sacrifices that the Americans faced at Valley Forge fostered resiliency in the struggling Continental Army. Martha's presence at Valley Forge nurtured and strengthened her husband to endure many additional years of danger, disappointment, and battle fatigue.

Martha at Newburgh and the "Purple Heart"

Other deadly engagements between the British Royal Army and the Continentals occurred during the ensuing years following the Valley Forge encampment. Martha continued to join her husband at many Continental Army winter encampments. The final and lengthiest Continental Army encampment was in New York State. Following the stunning victory over the British at Yorktown, in October 1781, the bulk of the Americans were encamped at the New Windsor Cantonment, in today's Vails Gate, Orange County, NY. Here 7,000 restless Continental soldiers were stationed for 17 months. General Washington established his final command headquarters in Newburgh at the Jonathan Hasbrouck House, a small, multi-room "Dutch-style" stone-covered structure situated on a steep bluff strategically overlooking the Hudson River. This modest house provided Washington some physical distance—five miles--from the restless Continental Army officers and soldiers stationed at New Windsor.

At the New Windsor Cantonment, General Washington faced a mounting crisis. The contentious issues included: (1) not receiving back pay; (2) being denied the full amount of pensions previously promised; and (3) being ignored by the Continental Congress in Philadelphia. On March 10, 1783, General Washington was informed of a potential mutiny. Leading the uprising was Major General Horatio Gates and Major John Armstrong, Jr. They planned to take troops to Philadelphia and demand redress of contentious issues. Washington interceded before the march on Philadelphia took place. On March 15, the Commander-in-Chief faced Gates, Armstrong, and the other discontented Continental Army officers at the "Temple" building in New Windsor. After delivering a speech, known as the "Newburgh Address," Washington began reading a letter. He needed the assistance of spectacles in order to read the small handwriting on the letter. As he put on the spectacles, Washington uttered the following words: "Gentlemen, you must pardon me. I have grown gray in your service and now find myself growing blind." These words, a poignant addendum to his "Newburgh Address," were spoken with sincerity and humility. Washington brought his officers to tears, and tensions at Newburgh immediately eased. No mutinous march on Philadelphia would occur. Peace would come to the United States of America with the signing of the "Treaty of Paris" on September 3, 1783.

Aside from being the longest and last encampment of the Continental Army, the Newburgh headquarters is noted for another milestone in American military history. It was at Newburgh that General Washington authorized an award for enlisted soldiers called the "Badge of Military Merit." The insignia was made with purple and white embroidered cloth shaped in the form of a heart to be worn over an honored soldier's heart. The "Merit" badge is on permanent display at Washington's Newburgh Headquarters and is considered the forerunner of the "Purple Heart" military decoration that was authorized on April 5, 1917 by the U.S. Congress for those wounded in the First World War and thereafter. Martha Washington was an expert seamstress during the time the sewn-cloth decoration with the embroidered word: "Merit" was first seen. This writer searched for a linkage between Martha and the "Badge of Military Merit." However, no linkage was found. Nevertheless, in the heart of this appreciative scribe, Martha and the "Merit" badge should be shown together because she, in many respects, deserved this great honor.

Portrait of Martha Washington; the embroidered "Badge of Military Merit"; and the "Purple Heart" medal that was authorized on April 5, 1917 and thereafter for those wounded in battle.

Washington Headquarters, Newburgh, NY

Acknowledging the historical importance of General Washington's Newburgh headquarters, the State of New York purchased the Hasbrouck House and surrounding acreage in 1850. It was the first time in United States history that a government entity would designate a house or site an "official historic place." In 1961, the house and sprawling site that extends east to the Hudson River became a U.S. National Park Service administered landmark formally called: "Washington's Headquarters, Newburgh, NY" (from which information and photographs used in this essay were obtained). During the Revolutionary War, from 1775 through 1783, George Washington spent more time in New York than in any other state. While Washington served as Commander-in-Chief, U.S. president, and again as a gentleman farmer, Martha was his indispensable lady. They were married for more than 40 years. Martha passed away at Mount Vernon on May 22, 1802--eleven days before her 71st birthday.

General George Washington's Headquarters,
State Historic Site.

Chapter 9
Major General Anthony Wayne:
"Mad" Warrior at the Battles of Stony Point and Fallen Timbers

Covering areas within Rockland and Orange Counties, Harriman State Park is the second largest facility in the New York State Park System. The highlight of this Empire State park is the Anthony Wayne Recreation Area (see photograph below).

Why was this American general called "Mad" Anthony Wayne? Born on January 1, 1745, Wayne sensed at an early age that his destiny would be related to leadership in battle. Growing up in Chester County, Pennsylvania, Wayne enjoyed a comfortable life at the 500-acre Waynesborough estate that was inherited by his father, Isaac Wayne, in the early 1700's. Anthony was schooled in the arts and sciences at the College of Philadelphia that is the present day University of Pennsylvania. An excellent student in mathematics, he subsequently became a surveyor. In this role, Wayne developed stamina for rigorous outdoor life. At the same time, he met influential individuals, such as the most famous Philadelphian,

Benjamin Franklin.

With this connection, Wayne was asked to join an association that in 1764 purchased land in Nova Scotia for a new colony. Wayne served as agent and surveyor for these newly purchased lands. After a year in Nova Scotia, Wayne returned to Pennsylvania and began courting Mary "Polly" Penrose, the daughter of prominent Philadelphia merchant, Bartholomew Penrose. They were married on March 25, 1766. The newlyweds settled into the Waynesborough family estate, where Anthony farmed and opened a tanning business while still surveying for clients. In 1774, Wayne began a lifelong joint career in politics and in the military. He was elected to represent Chester County at the Pennsylvania Provincial Convention that year. The purpose of this gathering was to formulate a response to Great Britain's heavy-handed treatment of its American colonies and specifically to the martial law imposed upon Boston's citizens. On January 2, 1776, Wayne was unanimously recommended by the Pennsylvania Committee of Safety to the rank of Colonel of the 4th Battalion of the Pennsylvanian line. On the next day, the Continental Congress also voted its approval for Wayne at this rank.

Battles of Brandywine, Paoli, and Valley Forge

In late 1776, following his demonstrated leadership at the Battle of Trois-Rivières (Three Rivers) in Quebec, Canada, Anthony Wayne was promoted to Brigadier General by the Continental Congress on February 21, 1777. He was assigned the command of Fort Ticonderoga in the New York State frontier. However, Wayne found nothing but hardship at the fort with inadequate food, clothing, and war materiel. He was glad to be relieved of his duties at the fort in mid-May 1777. Wayne then served with distinction at the Battles of Brandywine and Germantown, occurring on September 11 and October 4, 1777, respectively. Between these battles, however, Wayne came under harsh criticism for inadequately protecting his troops camped at the Village of Paoli. What came to be known as the "Paoli Massacre" occurred on the evening of September 20, 1777. Overnight, the British stormed the American

Patriot camp and bayoneted hundreds of unprepared Continental soldiers. Always protective of his reputation, Wayne demanded a court martial from Commander-in-Chief George Washington in order to clear his name. Wayne did indeed achieve this objective with the court martial board concluding a verdict of "not guilty" on November 1. Furthermore, the court martial board commended Wayne as "an active, brave, and vigilant officer." Wayne next served with distinction at the Valley Forge encampment during the arduous winter and spring of 1778. On June 28 of that year, Brigadier General Wayne and his Pennsylvania regiment performed admirably at the Battle of Monmouth Courthouse in northern New Jersey. This large-scale engagement at first resembled a rout of the Americans until General George Washington rallied the troops. Ultimately, this massive battle proved to be indecisive, in that neither army forced the retreat of the other army from the field. With temperatures hovering around 100 degrees Fahrenheit, the heat killed nearly as many soldiers as did battle wounds. However, this event proved that the Americans were willing to fight, head-on, against the best of the British Royal Army.

Emmanuel Gottlieb Leutze's 1854 painting:
"Washington Rallying the Troops at the Battle of Monmouth, June 28, 1778."

Statue of Brigadier General Anthony Wayne at Valley Forge Historical Park, Pennsylvania.

Wayne's Raid at Stony Point

Of even greater significance to Wayne's stellar military career was his carefully planned and successfully executed raid at a British-held fort north of New-York City called Stony Point. General Washington was reluctant to deplete the strength of the Continental Army by diverting troops to attack the British-held fort at Stony Point. Thus, the General-in-Chief positioned the bulk of his army further to the north of this fort at West Point, which lies at the strategic double-bend of the Hudson River. However, Wayne saw a significant benefit in taking Stony Point and requested permission from General Washington to undertake a raid there. Washington assented. On the night of July 15, 1779, Wayne commenced the raid by his Pennsylvania regiment. This surprise bayonet attack on Stony Point, which juts out to form a point over the Hudson River, was a complete victory. For many, Wayne's raid on the British encampment was in some ways seen as "payback" for the "Paoli Massacre" perpetrated by the British one year earlier.

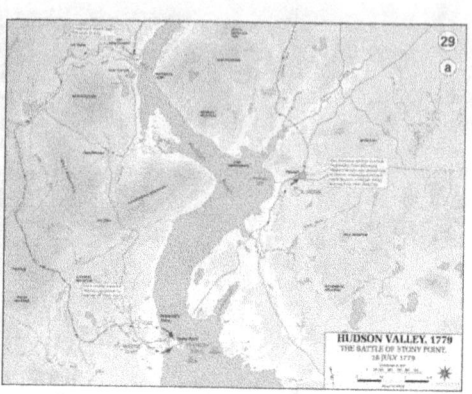

Map of the Stony Point garrison raid on the night of July 15-16, 1779. Notice the point of land jutting out into the Hudson River at the bottom of the map.

On July 18, 1778, General Washington rode to the now Continental Army-held Stony Point fort and shook the hands of the men who successfully stormed and defeated the British. Major General Baron von Steuben was delighted that his "Light Infantry," who he personally trained previously at Valley Forge was victorious. Wayne's audacious raid, for which he earned the sobriquet "Mad," had a powerful impact on British General Henry Clinton. With the Americans occupying Stony Point, the British were unable to use the Hudson River to invade northern New York State. In a report in the *Annual Register of 1779*, Secretary of the French legation, Conrad Alexandre Gérard, wrote about the assault on Stony Point as follows: "It would have done honor to the most veteran soldiers...Plan, execution, courage, address and energy, in short, the most rare qualities were found united there, and I am convinced that this action will elevate the ideas of Europe about the military qualities of the Americans."

Battle of Yorktown, Promotion to Major General, and Financial Troubles

From late 1779 through the beginning of 1781, Wayne commanded troops in New Jersey and New York. Life at these various encampments was tedious and, at times, precarious. On January 1, 1781, soldiers of the Pennsylvania line mutinied for lack of food, clothing, and pay. These unacceptable conditions had lasted for over a year. After killing one of their officers and wounding two others, the mutineers marched to Philadelphia. Extremely tense negotiations ensued between the mutineers and the then President of Pennsylvania, Joseph Reed. Fortunately, with almost all of the mutineers' demands being met, including a general amnesty for the rebellious soldiers themselves, the mutiny ended. In mid-1781, Wayne continued to serve as the commander of the Pennsylvanian line under the overall leadership of Major General Nathanael Greene and, at times, under the command of Gilbert du Motier, Marquis de La Fayette. By July of that year, Wayne and his troops were constantly on the move further south in Virginia, North Carolina, South Carolina, and Georgia. In September and October 1781, Wayne's regiment directly participated in the massive victory over the British at Yorktown, Virginia. General George Lord Cornwallis and his British Royal Army were now defeated.

However, Native American Creek and Cherokee tribes were still at war with the new nation. To resolve this matter, Wayne was ordered to sever any British alliances with these tribes. For his esteemed leadership and services while leading his troops in Georgia, Wayne was granted a sprawling rice plantation that was called "Richmond." In the closing days of the Revolutionary War in fall 1783, Wayne was promoted to the rank of Major General in the Continental Army. After the war, Wayne turned his energies toward Pennsylvanian politics. After several unsuccessful attempts, Wayne was finally elected to the U.S. Congress in 1791. His tenure there lasted only six months because Congress voted to overturn the election results due to voting irregularities. His political troubles, however, paled in comparison to his financial difficulties as the result of several failed business ventures. Creditors seeking to arrest him for non-payment threatened him with debtors' prison. As a consequence, Wayne was forced to stay away from his native state as much as possible in order to be out of reach of his Philadelphia creditors. By 1792, Wayne recovered financially due to the lucrative sale of his Georgia plantation. Unfortunately, at this time, his health was rapidly deteriorating due to recurring bouts of fevers as well as pain from an extreme case of gout in his arms and legs.

Wayne Organizes and Takes Command of the "Legion Army"

The Treaty of Paris in 1783 ended hostilities between Great Britain and the new United States of America. However, the treaty had little effect in stopping the continual bloodshed occurring in the Old Northwest Territories of the new nation. This area encompasses large parts of the present-day states of Illinois, Indiana, Michigan, and Ohio. Native American tribes were continually agitated by the defeated, though still ever-present, British troops in these Territories. The Native Americans were fiercely defending their ancestral tribal lands from encroachment by American settlers from the original thirteen colonies fanning out westward. Intense, years-long negotiations between Miami tribal Chief Michinikwa ("Little Turtle"), who led the Native American tribal confederation, and Washington Administration emissaries ended in failure. In 1790, Brevet Brigadier General Josiah Harmar led U.S. troops in fighting "Little Turtle" and the Native American confederation. This attempt was a defeat for the U.S. troops. A year later, Major General Arthur St. Clair led U.S. troops in a second effort that failed as well. Frustrated by these failures, President George Washington assigned Major General Anthony Wayne to make yet another attempt. Wayne carefully organized, trained, and equipped his troops that he named the "Legion Army." Through discipline and resolve, the "Legion Army" was a powerful fighting force that consisted of ground troops, mounted soldiers, and artillery that was combined into one cohesive military unit. Under the superlative leadership of Wayne, the "Legion Army" defeated "Little Turtle" and his confederation on August 20, 1794 at the Battle of Fallen Timbers. ("Fallen Timbers" was the name given to this wooded region due to the many felled trees from an earlier hurricane.)

Defeated in battle and denied further support by the British, the Native American tribal leaders had no choice other than to sign the Treaty of Greenville on August 3, 1795 at Fort Greenville--located in Ohio, which became a state in 1803. (Wayne named the treaty and the fort after his military colleague and close friend Nathanael Greene, who died from heatstroke in Georgia on June 19, 1786.) By the terms of the Treaty of Greenville, the Native American confederation ceded vast territories to the U.S.A. in return for various forms of compensation from the federal government.

Major General Anthony Wayne
in his Continental Army uniform.

Last Years and Legacies

Following the 1795 signing of the treaty, Wayne returned home to widespread acclaim but in poor health. Wayne also had to contend with his disloyal second-in-command, Brigadier General James Wilkinson. Unknown to Wayne, Wilkinson was sending a steady stream of letters to President George Washington criticizing Wayne's ability to command. Washington was well aware of Wayne's abilities and summarily disregarded Wilkinson's poison-pen letters. In the decades hence—far too late to relieve Wayne of his disloyal second-in-command officer--evidence was uncovered that directly implicated Wilkinson in several questionable activities. Wilkinson was twice the Senior Officer of the U.S. Army and was appointed the first Governor of the Louisiana Territory. During the War of 1812, he led at two battles that were complete defeats for the Americans. Following his death in 1825, it was discovered that Wilkinson was a paid agent of the Spanish crown! This damning evidence was revealed about Wilkinson long after it could have enabled Wayne to remove this traitorous army officer from his military staff. Wilkinson's reputation in U.S. history has been abysmal. The condemnation against Wilkinson includes Theodore Roosevelt's vitriol in *The Winning of the West* (1889). The future U.S. president excoriates Wilkinson as follows: "In all our history, there is no more despicable character" (p. 124). Wayne could not rely upon his untrustworthy second-in-command to act appropriately in his absence administrating the Old Northwest Territories. Thus, Wayne was obliged to repeatedly journey to these frontier regions to properly attend to matters. Returning from a Detroit military base during one such trip, he took violently ill with a raging fever at Presque Island near today's Erie, Pennsylvania. Wayne died there on December 15, 1796.

Anthony Wayne has been widely recognized for his leadership and valor in battle. Many U.S. cities, communities, counties, forests and parks, rivers, schools and colleges, streets and highways, and towns and villages are named after him. Hollywood moguls were unhappy having their cowboy film star with the name Marion Morrison. Based on Anthony Wayne's heroic reputation, the actor was renamed "John Wayne." "Wayne" was also used for the comic book superhero Bruce Wayne a.k.a. "Batman." The extreme bravery and derring-do Anthony Wayne demonstrated on numerous battlefield engagements—especially at the raid at Stony Point--earned him the sobriquet: "Mad." When one visits the Anthony Wayne Recreation Area in New York's second largest park, it would be most fitting to remember what this American hero accomplished!

Pastel portrait of Major General Anthony Wayne by James Sharples, Sr., 1796. Independence NHP.

Reference

Nelson, P. D. (1985). *Anthony Wayne: Soldier of the Early Republic*. Bloomington, IN: Indiana Press.

Roosevelt, T. (1889). *The Winning of the West, Volume III: The Founding of the Trans-Allegheny Commonwealths, 1784-1790*. http://www.theodorerooseveltcenter.org/en/Research/Digital-Library/Record.aspx?libID=o288640; Theodore Roosevelt Digital Library. Dickinson State University).

Chapter 10
Major General Oliver Otis Howard: Civil War Hero, Peacemaker, and Founder of Howard University and Lincoln Memorial University

Oliver Otis Howard commanded Union Army troops, many from New York, which sent the most soldiers into combat of any state during the Civil War. Amidst the Peninsular Campaign defeat for the Union Army, Howard achieved a stunning victory at the Battle of Fair Oaks. Howard paid dearly at that battle; he was twice shot in his right arm necessitating an amputation. For his bravery, he was awarded the U.S. Congressional Medal of Honor. After the war, he served as Commissioner of the Freedmen's Bureau. In this important role, Howard helped former enslaved African Americans in obtaining an education, healthcare, and preparation for career positions. He displayed integrity and dogged tenacity fending off constant attacks from racists—from the North as well as the South—who disgracefully opposed aiding African Americans. Howard doggedly overcame bureaucratic and racial obstacles to create Howard University, a premier academic institution. Located in the nation's capital, HU has thrived in the preparation of professionals in a wide variety of fields.

Thirty-three years later, after the retired general accumulated considerable wealth from book, magazine, and speech royalties, Howard fulfilled Lincoln's request by donating substantial funds to establish Lincoln Memorial University located at the Cumberland Gap town of Harrogate, Tennessee. Howard was known for his humane beliefs and indisputable integrity as "The Christian General."

Early Life of "Otis" Howard

Though he is best known as U.S. Army Major General O. O. Howard, during his early life, friends and family called him: "Otis." He was born in Leeds, Maine, on November 8, 1830 to a large family. Some of his relatives lived in Peekskill, New York. Otis' father, Rowland Bailey Howard, would regularly visit his New York relatives. On one visit in 1835, Rowland returned to Maine with a young African American boy named Edward Johnson. Otis and the young lad from New York State's Hudson Valley were close in age, temperamentally similar, and brotherly in feeling. Sadly, his father and his best friend, Edward, would both die before Otis reached the age of 10. In his 1907 autobiography, Howard wrote that his close relationship with Edward Johnson "relieved me from that feeling of prejudice which would have hindered me from doing the work of the Freedmen" (p. 13). Otis' mother, Eliza Otis Howard, was a staunch believer in education as a means by which her sons could become professionals and forego the drudgery of farm life. She sent Otis to school beginning at age four. Five years later, he began attending Monmouth Academy. At age 9, he was many years younger than his secondary school-level classmates. Otis was an excellent student. At age 16, he was admitted to Bowdoin College—one of Maine's preeminent higher learning institutions. Otis graduated from Bowdoin in 1850. That same year, at age 19, he was accepted to the U.S. Military Academy at West Point. Howard treasured this military academy. At various times in his life, Howard was a cadet, instructor, and superintendent at this Orange County, New York, military institution. In 1854, he graduated fourth in his class of 43 at West Point and was commissioned a Brevet Second Lieutenant. He was first stationed at the Watervliet Arsenal in Troy just east of the New York State capital at Albany. In 1855, he married Elizabeth Anne Waite, with whom he had seven children. Two years later, Howard was transferred to Florida, then in the midst of the Third

Seminole War. Here, he experienced at a Methodist revival meeting a "religious awakening" that changed his perspective on life. From this time forward, Howard was devoutly religious and later became widely known during the Civil War as the "The Christian General."

Valor During the Civil War

The Civil War commenced in April 1861. On May 29, the governor of his native state appointed Howard the colonel of the 3rd Maine Infantry Regiment. Fifty-three days later, his regiment was drawn into combat at the First Battle of Bull Run. This battle was the first of many losses by the Union Army during the early years of the war. Less than a year later, he was promoted to brigadier general and was put in command of the 61st New York Regiment. Overall, the Peninsular Campaign of spring 1862 in Virginia is considered a setback for the Union Army. However, one component of the campaign was a stunning success: the Battle of Fair Oaks. Here, Howard led the charge of the New York troops overwhelming Confederate entrenchments. During this engagement, Howard was shot in his right wrist and minutes later his right elbow with Minié balls. These wounds required amputation of his arm. For his valor and leadership under fire, Howard was awarded the U.S. Congressional Medal of Honor. His citation reads in part: "With bravery and total disregard for his own safety, Brigadier General O. O. Howard led the 61st New York Infantry Regiment in a charge at Fair Oaks, Virginia, in which he was twice severely wounded in the right arm, necessitating amputation on 1 June 1862." Howard returned to his command less than three months later at the end of August 1862 at the Second Battle of Bull Run--unfortunately yet another loss for the Union Army. Three weeks later, Howard replaced seriously wounded Major General John Sedgwick at the Battle of Antietam on September 17, 1862. With a combined North and South death toll of 22,717, more Americans were killed on this day than on any other day in history, even taking into account the World Wars of the 20th century. Though with a steep cost in lives, Antietam was marginally, though crucially, a victory for the Union Army of the Potomac.

In spring 1863, Howard was promoted to Brevet Major General--a temporary rank for the duration of the war. He replaced Major General Franz Sigel, commander of the Union Army XI Corps. Sigel was considered a "political general," who was appointed based on his ability to recruit German-American troops. Following several battlefield calamitous losses where his command skills were questioned, Sigel was reassigned as a commander to a smaller number of troops. Insulted by this, Sigel resigned his commission. Many immigrants, especially from Ireland and Germany, fought in the Union Army and, to a lesser extent, in the Confederate Army during the Civil War. However, the Union Army XI Corps was unique in that far more than half of its soldiers were comprised of first-generation German immigrants from New-York City and second-generation German Americans from Ohio. As such, the XI Corps was nicknamed "The Flying Dutchmen," whose slogan was: "I fights *mit* Sigel." When Howard, a New England Yankee, was assigned to command the XI Corps, these *Deutsche* troops were bitterly resentful. However, they and many others would soon change their view of the one-armed general, who consistently displayed his bravery at the Battles at Chancellorsville, Gettysburg, and Atlanta.

Photograph of Brevet Major General Howard,
who lost his right arm during the American Civil War.

On May 2, 1863, Confederate Major General Thomas "Stonewall" Jackson and his Rebel soldiers surprised, outflanked, and nearly decimated the Union Army of the Potomac at Chancellorsville, Virginia. Major General Joseph "Fighting Joe" Hooker was in command of several corps. This included "The Flying Dutchmen" XI Corps, positioned to the extreme west of the Union Army of the Potomac. The XI Corps was the first to be attacked by Jackson's Rebels emerging from the Spotsylvania County woodland known as "The Wilderness." (This battle took place at the same location but is separate from the "Battle of the Wilderness," which occurred a year later on May 5 to 7, 1864.) At the 1863 Battle of Chancellorsville, the XI Corps sustained 20 percent casualties including Hooker, who was knocked unconscious for over an hour when a cannon ball burst nearby. In the aftermath of this largest defeat of the Union Army, Hooker blamed the defeat on his subordinate generals—especially Howard for not being sufficiently prepared to fend off Jackson's attack. The topic of who is to blame for the Chancellorsville defeat has been debated incessantly. In 2013, in an attempt to settle the issue, the U.S. Army Center of Military History prepared an extensive report, which analyzed all aspects of the battle. In the report's conclusion, Hooker was directly blamed for the defeat as being outgeneraled by Robert E. Lee and "Stonewall" Jackson. Furthermore, O. O. Howard was cited for his bravery: "General Howard, who had just returned from escorting one of his brigades to the fighting at Catharine Furnace, attempted his own heroic efforts to halt the rout of the XI Corps. The one-armed general grabbed a unit standard and galloped down the Orange Turnpike, encouraging his men to rally" (Bradford A. Wineman, 2013, p. 31-32). At this battle, Howard led again at the *front* of his troops. Unlike at the Battle of Fairs Oaks where he was wounded, Howard miraculously emerged without additional injury at the Battle of Chancellorsville. Surpassing the gore at Chancellorsville was the Battle of Gettysburg.

From July 1 to 3, 1863, Americans from the North killed Americans from the South in record-breaking numbers. The three-day death toll was: 51,000! During day one, Confederate Lieutenant General R. E. Lee led the Army of Northern Virginia in overrunning this small Pennsylvanian town. Attempting to halt Lee's advance was Major General John Fulton Reynolds—commander of the left wing of the Union Army of the Potomac. Within an hour after the battle ensued, a Confederate sharpshooter mortally wounded Reynolds in the upper neck. Brevet Major General Howard then assumed overall command of the Army of the Potomac and led an organized, fighting retreat three miles south of Gettysburg to Cemetery Hill. Though the "Bluecoats" were routed that day, Howard's expertise in repositioning the troops to Cemetery Hill was highly praised. At this defensive location, Union forces were able to repel wave after wave of Rebel attacks. On day two, the Union Army was victorious defending various positions on high ground that formed a backwards and upside down letter "J." The 20th Maine Infantry Regiment defended their position on "Little Round Top" until running out of ammunition. At that point, instead of retreating, their commander, Colonel (later Brevet Major General) Joshua Lawrence Chamberlain, a Bowdoin College professor "on sabbatical to study foreign languages in Europe," led his Maine troops in a successful "rotating spoke" bayonet charge against the Rebels. For his bravery and leadership, Chamberlain was awarded the U.S. Congressional Medal of Honor. By the end of day three at the Battle of Gettysburg, following the gallant but futile "Pickett's Charge" of the Confederate Army, the "Bluecoats" had routed Lee's Army of Northern Virginia.

Major General William Tecumseh Sherman and his staff (from left to right): O. O. Howard, John A. Logan, William B. Hazen, Sherman, Jefferson C. Davis, Henry W. Slocum, Joseph A. Mower, and Frank Blair.

In 1864, Howard was assigned to Union Major General William Tecumseh Sherman's Army of the West. Howard played a significant role in the decisive victory at the Battle of Atlanta and in "Sherman's March to the Sea" ("March thru Georgia"). Howard's troops fought in Sherman's thrust north through South Carolina and North Carolina in early 1865. Sherman later assessed his second-in-command's bravery and leadership as follows: "O. O. Howard was a Corps commander of the utmost skill, nicety, and precision." At the end of the war, Howard returned to his permanent rank of Brigadier General. It would take 21 more years before he was promoted to the permanent rank of Major General.

Freedmen's Bureau Commissioner and Washington, D.C. Turmoil

After Lincoln's assassination in April 1865, Vice President Andrew Johnson was sworn-in as president. A month later, the U.S. Army established the Bureau of Refugees, Freedmen, and Abandoned Lands—better known as the "Freedmen's Bureau." Many generals sought and were considered for the role of Commissioner. Abolitionist Reverend Henry Ward Beecher, pastor of the Plymouth Church in Brooklyn (also called the

"Grand Central Station of the Underground Railroad"), adamantly supported Howard for this position. In Beecher's view, Howard was eminently qualified for this important task based on his long-term advocacy for abolition, civil rights equality, and exceptional integrity. Howard got the job but had little time to celebrate. He had to deal immediately with a mountain of arduous problems. Adding to his difficulties was President Andrew Johnson, an overt racist, who bitterly opposed the founding purpose for which the Freedmen's Bureau was established. Johnson was a partisan Democrat, who vehemently disagreed with the Radical Republicans in the U.S. Congress. Johnson also strongly disagreed with Secretary of War Edwin McMasters Stanton over Reconstruction measures being implemented by the U.S. Army in the South. When word leaked out that Johnson intended to fire Edwin Stanton, the U.S. Congress hurriedly passed the "Tenure of Office Act" on March 3, 1867. When asked to sign this law, Johnson immediately issued a veto and then attempted to remove Stanton from office. These actions irked congressional Republicans, who then initiated impeachment proceedings. For violating laws duly passed by the U.S. Congress and for impeding Reconstruction efforts, Johnson was impeached in the U.S. House of Representatives. By one vote, Johnson narrowly avoided a "conviction" of his impeachment in the U.S. Senate.

Amidst the political turmoil occurring in the nation's capital, Howard was tasked with assisting millions of former slaves yearning for, and fully owed, integration into American society. In 1865, Howard stated:

> The rights of the freedman, which are not yet secured to him, are the direct reverse of the wrongs committed against him. I never could conceive how a man could become a better laborer by being made to carry an over heavy and wearisome burden which in no way facilitates his work. I never could detect the shadow of a reason why the color of the skin should impair the right to life, liberty, and the pursuit of justice.

Regrettably, by the end of Howard's nine tumultuous years as Commissioner, many of his accomplishments on behalf of the Freedmen were diminished and some were wholly negated. Reconstruction Era commentators have blamed Howard for attempting too much and accomplishing too little. This criticism may have some validity, because Howard did indeed attempt too many tasks at the same time. To further add to the confusion, the highly contentious 1876 U.S. presidential election had the potential of igniting another civil war. In avoiding another widespread conflict, the U.S. Congress entered into a compromise. Ohio Republican Rutherford Birchard Hayes would become president but Reconstruction measures—many of critical necessity to former enslaved Americans--would terminate. The end result of this bargain was that "The North won the Civil War but lost the peace!"

Dealings with Native Americans

On March 7, 1872, Howard took a leave of absence from the Freedmen's Bureau to undertake a temporary assignment leading the U.S. Army battling the Apaches led by Chief Cochise. "The Christian General" viewed his task more broadly than solely to "kill Indians." While willing to battle Cochise, Howard was also willing to make peace with Cochise and thus prevent a deadly war with the Apaches. Historian John A. Carpenter (1999) describes Howard's first peacemaking event as follows:

> ...He [Howard] met Thomas J. Jeffords a well-known scout who, it was reputed, was the only white man accepted by [Apache Chief] Cochise. At first Jeffords was somewhat prejudiced against General Howard because, as he later said, 'Howard was only posing as a Christian soldier.' Jeffords soon changed his view when Howard told him he would be perfectly willing to go to Cochise in the Indian's stronghold without military escort. Of all the Indians of the Southwest at the time none had a bloodier record than Cochise, none had as notorious a reputation for taking vengeance on all white men. The soldier who would walk straight into the

enemy's country might be a little foolhardy but he was also brave. Jeffords now knew his man and set about making the arrangements for this hazardous expedition (p. 214).

After gaining the trust of Cochise, Howard was able to achieve lasting amity with the Apache Tribal Nations with a peace treaty signed on October 12, 1872. However, the Christian General could not readily achieve peace with the Nez Perce tribes in 1874. These Native Americans populated portions of today's states of Oregon, Washington, and Idaho. In particular, Howard was tasked with persuading Chief Joseph to relocate his Nez Perce tribes to a new reservation. Relocation was unacceptable in and of itself but especially undesirable in this case because the new reservation territory was smaller in size. Chief Joseph understandably refused, and widespread warfare broke out between the Nez Perce tribes and the U.S. Army. On October 5, 1877, Chief Joseph and a portion of the Nez Perce tribe were defeated in battle and forced to surrender to Howard. However, the remainder of the Nez Perce warriors continued to fight until July 28, 1878. All told, the Nez Perce tribe suffered a tremendous loss of life and, in the end, lost its homeland territory. Though Howard was credited as the victorious general of this "Indian War," news reporters and later commentators on Native American affairs have justifiably excoriated the U.S. government and Howard over dealings with the Nez Perce tribes. In particular, Chief Joseph specifically criticized Howard for being too precipitous in dealing with the Nez Perce. According to Chief Joseph, had Howard waited, war could have been avoided.

On January 21, 1881, Howard began serving as Superintendent of the Military Academy at West Point. In May of that year, American author Mark Twain visited West Point to participate in the 100th anniversary celebration of the British Army surrender at Yorktown. During this visit, Twain and Howard became close friends. Twain encouraged Howard to follow in his footsteps as a writer and speechmaker. With Twain's encouragement and Howard's innate ability, the general subsequently flourished as a successful author and highly sought-after public speaker. During his tenure at the military academy, Howard made several reforms that included the cessation of cadet "hazing" for disciplinary infractions. Unfortunately, following his tenure at "The Point," these harsh tactics re-emerged. From 1882 to 1886, Howard served as commander of the U.S. Army Department of the Platte. In 1884, the French government made him a "Chevalier of the Legion of Honor." On April 2, 1886, the U.S. Senate approved his promotion to "Major General of the United States Army." Howard's next assignment, until 1888, was as Head of the Military Division of the Pacific. In November of that year, Howard was appointed commander of the Military Division of the Atlantic. His vast area of authority now included Arkansas and all states east of the Mississippi River except Illinois. The 58-year old general chose as his headquarters location Governors Island in New-York Harbor. His held this position for six years and retired in November 1894.

Photograph of Major General Howard taken in 1908 — one year before his death.

Oliver Otis Howard entered the U.S. Army as an academy cadet in New York State, and 44 years later retired while being stationed in New York State. He died in Burlington, Vermont, on October 26, 1909, thirteen days shy of his 79th birthday. Howard nobly earned the title: "The Christian General." He strove against injustice. One is reminded of Rev. Martin Luther King, Jr.'s most enduring written message. In his letter sent from jail to Joe C. Higginbotham, Rev. King explains why a minister from Atlanta, Georgia, had to lead a protest march against injustice in Birmingham, Alabama. The selfless minister stated: "...Injustice anywhere is a threat to justice everywhere. We are caught in an inescapable network of mutuality, tied in a single garment of destiny. Whatever affects one directly affect all indirectly."

References

Carpenter, J. A. (1999). *Sword and Olive Branch: Oliver Otis Howard*. NY: Fordham University Press.

Howard, O. O. (1907). *Autobiography of Oliver Otis Howard, Major General, United States Army*. NY: Baker & Taylor.

King, M. L. Jr. (April 16, 1963). Letter from a Birmingham jail.

Wineman, B. A. (2013). *The Chancellorsville Campaign January-May 1863*. U.S. Army Center of Military History.

www.ingramcontent.com/pod-product-compliance
Lightning Source LLC
Chambersburg PA
CBHW070547170426
43201CB00012B/1754